SOLDIERS' VERSE

VERSES CHOSEN BY PATRIC DICKINSON

WITH
ORIGINAL LITHOGRAPHS
BY
WILLIAM SCOTT

GRANGER POETRY LIBRARY

GRANGER BOOK CO., INC.
Great Neck, N.Y.

First Published 1945
Reprinted 1979

International Standard Book Number
0-89609-157-0

Library of Congress Catalog Number
79-50841

Printed in the United States of America

INTRODUCTION

My dear Vin,

In one of your letters from your prison camp you spoke of "the freedom of a limitation"—a phrase that has been often recalled during the collection of this anthology. Another which constantly returned was from Yeats:

> I think it better that in times like these
> A poet's tongue be silent.

Love, War, and Death were the three subjects for Poetry according to Dante. Love and Death still keep their timelessness but War owing to the development of its mechanical aids has altered its perspective. In Hannibal's time you could have begun a poem on the siege of Saguntum "O War . . ." and there'd have been no necessity to mention a ballista. Whilst war-in-poetry could be generally expressed, or be the spring of catholic human emotion, it remained poetic material. The Napoleonic wars to the Romantics really meant Odes on Liberty, Addresses to Freedom, and attacks on Tyranny. The Crimean War or the Boer War for these reasons did not inspire poets at all, with the exception of "The Charge of the Light Brigade," and the ballads and broadsheets of the period do not happen to fit in here. The Great 1914-18 War is the only war in which poetry has been written on the subject of war, and moreover on behalf of the soldiers who wage it. The Total War of 1939-45 has naturally produced very little War-poetry. For as the scope of war has enlarged the scope of poetry has diminished. The small incident engrosses the poet. It is one of the horrors of our time that tragedy has become commonplace, almost banal.

Our warfare: its bombs and rockets and the whole ghastly paraphernalia of death is not directly assimilable into poetry. You may make symbols of it but once you are among its terms poetry seems to desert you or at best becomes a sort of conscript prose in poetic uniform. But War-poems of previous centuries can have little significance to us now as War-poems—they may be good, or bad poems, but they no longer apply to war as we know it. These problems must lead to a series of limitations: in time, in actual subject, and of course in personal taste and reading.

I suppose there are only two ways of making anthologies: the inclusive British Museum method and the exclusive personal choice. This anthology at any rate is made out of poems which remain for me real poems—whatever one's definition of poetry may be, there's a basic, arbitrary, instinctive taste which directs and approves, or rejects. I think one of the chief justifications of anthologies is that the one limited to the printed page is set free by its companions in the head of the reader. An anthology should be provoking in this way. Of other personal limitations, you can't fail to notice that nearly all the poems are in a strict form and that they are complete in themselves and not extracted. These aren't the only poems about soldiers I have ever read or the only ones I like—they are the ones which happen to fit in with my plan for this anthology.

In those days when knowledge of the Classics was a *sine qua non* of the educated man and woman; when therefore we had a reasonable knowledge of our own language, two of the first words we had to learn and to decline were *Bellum*, War; and *Miles*, a Soldier. It was something of this spirit I thought that one should bring to an anthology of soldiers' verse. There should be poems both Vocative and Genitive as well as the general run of Nominative and Accusative poems in which '*miles gloriosus*' is subject or object. There should be a certain amount '*de re militari*', and a certain freedom within the strictness of the declension of *bellum* and *miles*. Out of this grew the idea that the whole anthology should be a sort of thematic declension—though its cases merge one into another and are not quite equivalent to the Latin ones.

So if you read through from beginning to end I hope you may derive some pleasure from these "cases". I know anthologies are primarily for dipping into and not for consecutive reading, but this fulfills a double purpose: you may choose, as it were, freedom or limitation.

The whole arrangement and, too, the immediate juxtapositions are not fortuitous. For example the R.L.S. rhyme placed after Browning's "Incident of the French Camp" or the Edmund Blunden "War Memorial 1914-1918" before the Dylan Thomas, succeed

SOLDIERS' VERSE

(I can only say for me) in making an effect the poems could not and did not try to achieve separately. You will discover many of these complements—you may find them stimulating, or irritating, but there is no need to find them at all.

Indeed it is this arrangement—immeasurably enhanced by William Scott's lithographs—which I hope will make this selection a genuinely New Excursion into English Verse. Take the whole road or stop by the wayside—you can do as you please and that's why I'd like to dedicate this Anthology of Soldiers' Verse to you, for five long years a prisoner-of-war.

P.D.

*The Acknowledgments
will be found on pages* 116 *and* 117.

SOLDIERS' VERSE

I

HILAIRE BELLOC b. 1870

THE PACIFIST

Pale Ebenezer thought it wrong to fight,
But Roaring Bill (who killed him) thought it right.

SIEGFRIED SASSOON b. 1886

ANCIENT HISTORY

Adam, a brown old vulture in the rain,
Shivered below his wind-whipped olive-trees;
Huddling sharp chin on scarred and scraggy knees,
He moaned and mumbled to his darkening brain;
'*He was the grandest of them all — was Cain*!
'A lion laired in the hills, that none could tire:
'Swift as a stag: a stallion of the plain,
'Hungry and fierce with deeds of huge desire.'

Grimly he thought of Abel, soft and fair—
A lover with disaster in his face,
And scarlet blossom twisted in bright hair.
'Afraid to fight; was murder more disgrace? . . .
'*God always hated Cain*' . . . He bowed his head—
The gaunt wild man whose lovely sons were dead.

SIR HENRY NEWBOLT 1862-1938

THE NON-COMBATANT

Among a race high-handed, strong of heart,
Sea-rovers, conquerors, builders in the waste,
He had his birth; a nature too complete,
Eager and doubtful, no man's soldier sworn
And no man's chosen captain; born to fail,
A name without an echo: yet he too
Within the cloister of his narrow days
Fulfilled the ancestral rights, and kept alive
The eternal fire; it may be, not in vain;
For out of those who dropped a downward glance
Upon the weakling huddled at his prayers,
Perchance some looked beyond him, and then first
Beheld the glory, and what shrine it filled,
And to what Spirit sacred: or perchance
Some heard him chanting, though but to himself,
The old heroic names: and went their way:
And hummed his music on the march to death.

A. H. CLOUGH 1819-1861

from

AMOURS DE VOYAGE

Will they fight? They say so. And will the French? I can hardly,
Hardly think so; and yet — He is come, they say, to Palo,
He is passed from Monterone, at Santa Severa
He hath laid up his guns. But the Virgin, the Daughter of Roma,
She hath despised thee and laughed thee to scorn, — the Daughter of Tiber,
She hath shaken her head and built barricades against thee!

Will they fight? I believe it. Alas! 'tis ephemeral folly,
Vain and ephemeral folly, of course, compared with pictures,
Statues, and antique gems! — Indeed: and yet indeed too,
Yet methought, in broad day did I dream, — tell it not in St. James's,
Whisper it not in thy courts, O Christ Church! — yet did I, waking,
Dream of a cadence that sings, *Si tombent nos jeunes héros, la Terre en produit de nouveaux contre vous tous prêts à se battre*;
Dreamt of great indignations and angers transcendental,
Dreamt of a sword at my side and a battle-horse underneath me.

SIDNEY KEYES 1922 - 1943

ADVICE FOR A JOURNEY

The drums mutter for war and soon we must begin
To seek the country where they say that joy
Springs flowerlike among the rocks, to win
The fabulous golden mountain of our peace.

O my friends, we are too young
For explorers, have no skill nor compass,
Nor even that iron certitude which swung
Our fathers at their self-fulfilling North.

So take no rations, remember not your homes—
Only the blind and stubborn hope to track
This wilderness. The thoughtful leave their bones
In windy foodless meadows of despair.

Never look back, nor too far forward search
For the white Everest of your desire;
The screes roll underfoot and you will never reach
Those brittle peaks which only clouds may walk.

Others have come before you. The immortal
Live like reflections and their frozen faces

Will give you courage to ignore the subtle
Sneer of the gentian and the iceworn pebble.

The fifes cry death and the sharp winds call.
Set your face to the rock; go on, go out
Into the bad lands of battle, into the cloud-wall
Of the future, my friends, and leave your fear.

Go forth, my friends, the raven is no sibyl;
Break the clouds' anger with your unchanged faces.
You'll find, maybe, the dream under the hill—
But never Canaan, nor any golden mountain.

A. H. CLOUGH 1819-1861

from
AMOURS DE VOYAGE

Dulce it is, and *decorum*, no doubt, for the country to fall, — to
Offer one's blood an oblation to Freedom, and die for the Cause; yet
Still, individual culture is also something, and no man
Finds quite distinct the assurance that he of all others is called on,
Or would be justified even, in taking away from the world that
Precious creature, himself. Nature sent him here to abide here,
Else why send him at all? Nature wants him still, it is likely;
On the whole, we are meant to look after ourselves; it is certain
Each has to eat for himself, digest for himself, and in general
Care for his own dear life, and see to his own preservation;
Nature's intentions, in most things uncertain, in this are decisive;
Which, on the whole, I conjecture the Romans will follow, and I shall.

So we cling to our rocks like limpets; Ocean may bluster,
Over and under and round us; we open our shells to imbibe our
Nourishment, close them again, and are safe, fulfilling the purpose
Nature intended, — a wise one, of course, and a noble, we doubt not.
Sweet it may be and decorous, perhaps, for the country to die; but,
On the whole, we conclude the Romans won't do it, and I shan't.

WALT WHITMAN 1819-1892

MANHATTAN ARMING

First, O songs, for a prelude,
Lightly strike on the stretched tympanum, pride and joy in my city,
How she led the rest to arms, how she gave the cue,
How at once with lithe limbs, unwaiting a moment, she sprang;
(O superb! O Manhattan, my own, my peerless!
O strongest you in the hour of danger, in crisis! O truer than steel!)
How you sprang — how you threw off the costumes of peace with indifferent hand;
How your soft opera-music changed, and the drum and fife were heard in their stead;
How you led to the war (that shall serve for our prelude, songs of soldiers),
How Manhattan drum-taps led.

Forty years had I in my city seen soldiers parading;
Forty years as a pageant, till unawares, the lady of this teeming and turbulent city,
Sleepless amid her ships, her houses, her incalculable wealth,
With her million children around her, suddenly,
At dead of night, at news from the south,
Incensed, struck with clinched hand the pavement.

A shock electric, the night sustained it,
Till with ominous hum our hive at daybreak poured out its myriads.

From the houses then and the workshops, and through all the doorways,
Leaped they tumultuous, and lo! Manhattan arming.

To the drum-taps prompt,
The young men falling in and arming;
The mechanics arming, (the trowel, the jack-plane, the blacksmith's hammer, tossed aside with precipitation),

The lawyer leaving his office and arming, the judge leaving the court,
The driver deserting his waggon in the street, jumping down, throwing the reins abruptly down on the horses' backs,
The salesman leaving the store, the boss, book-keeper, porter, all leaving;
Squads gather everywhere by common consent, and arm;
The new recruits, even boys, the old men show them how to wear their accoutrements, they buckle the straps carefully;
Outdoors arming, indoors arming, the flash of the musket-barrels;
The white tents cluster in camps, the armed sentries around, the sunrise cannon and again at sunset;
Armed regiments arrive every day, pass through the city, and embark from the wharves;
(How good they look, as they tramp down to the river, sweaty, with their guns on their shoulders!
How I love them! how I could hug them, with their brown faces, and their clothes and knapsacks covered with dust!)
The blood of the city up — armed! armed! the cry everywhere,
The flags flung out from the steeples of churches, and from all the public buildings and stores,
The tearful parting, the mother kisses her son, the son kisses his mother,
(Loth is the mother to part, yet not a word does she speak to detain him;)
The tumultuous escort, the ranks of policemen preceding, clearing the way,
The unpent enthusiasm, the wild cheers of the crowd for their favourites;
The artillery, the silent cannons bright as gold, drawn along, rumble lightly over the stones;
(Silent cannons, soon to cease your silence,
Soon unlimbered to begin the red business!)
All the mutter of preparation, all the determined arming,
The hospital service, the lint, bandages, and medicines,
The women volunteering for nurses, the work begun for in earnest, no mere parade now;

War! an armed race is advancing! the welcome for battle, no turning away;
War! be it weeks, months, or years, an armed race is advancing to welcome it.

Mannahatta a-march! — and it's O to sing it well!
It's O for a manly life in the camp.

And the sturdy artillery,
The guns, bright as gold, the work for giants, to serve well the guns:
Unlimber them! (no more as the past forty years for salutes for courtesies merely;
Put in something now besides powder and wadding).

And you, lady of ships! you, Mannahatta,
Old matron of this proud, friendly, turbulent city,
Often in peace and wealth you were pensive or covertly frowned amid all your children;
But now you smile with joy, exulting old Mannahatta!

WILLIAM WORDSWORTH 1770-1850
SONNET
1811

The power of Armies is a visible thing,
Formal, and circumscribed in time and space;
But who the limits of that power shall trace
Which a brave People into light can bring
Or hide, at will,— for freedom combating
By just revenge inflamed? No foot may chase,
No eye can follow, to a fatal place
That power, that spirit, whether on the wing
Like the strong wind, or sleeping like the wind
Within its awful caves. — From year to year
Springs this indigenous produce far and near;
No craft this subtle element can bind,
Rising like water from the soil, to find
In every nook a lip that it may cheer.

LIONEL JOHNSON 1867-1902

THE COMING OF WAR, 1889

Gather the people, for the battle breaks:
    From camping grounds above the valley,
Gather the men-at-arms, and bid them rally:
    Because the morn, the battle, wakes.
High throned above the mountains and the main,
Triumphs the sun: far down, the pasture plain
    To trampling armour shakes.

This was the meaning of those plenteous years,
    Those unarmed years of peace unbroken:
Flashing war crowns them! Now war's trump hath spoken
    This final glory in our ears.
The old blood of our pastoral fathers now
Riots about our heart, and through our brow:
    Their sons can have no fears.

This was our whispering and haunting dream,
    When cornfields flourished, red and golden:
When vines hung purple, nor could be witholden
    The radiant outburst of their stream.
Earth cried to us, that all her laboured store
Was ours: that she had more to give, and more:
    For nothing, did we deem?

We give her back the glory of this hour.
    O sun and earth! O strength and beauty!
We use you now, we thank you now: our duty
    We stand to do, mailed in your power.
A little people of a favoured land,
Helmed with the blessing of the morn we stand:
    Our life is at its flower.

Gather the people, let the battle break:
    An hundred peaceful years are over.
Now march each man to battle as a lover:

For him, whom death shall overtake!
Sleeping upon this field, about his gloom
Voices shall pierce, to thrill his sacred tomb,
   Of pride for his great sake.

With melody about us: heart and feet
   Responding to one mighty measure;
Glad with the splendour of an holy pleasure;
   Swayed, one and all, as wind sways wheat:
Answering the sunlight with our eyes aglow;
Serene, and, proud, and passionate, we go
   Through airs of morning sweet.

Let no man dare to be disheartened now!
   We challenge death beyond denial.
Against the host of death we make our trial:
   Lord God of Hosts! do thou,
Who gavest us the fulness of thy sun
On fields of peace, perfect war's work begun:
   Warriors, to thee we bow.

O life-blood of remembrance! Long ago
   This land upheld our ancient fathers:
And for this land, their land, our land, now gathers
   One fellowship against the foe.
The spears flash: be they as our mothers' eyes!
The trump sounds: hearken to our fathers' cries!
   March we to battle so.

II

ALAN SEEGER 1888-1916

I HAVE A RENDEZVOUS WITH DEATH

    I have a rendezvous with Death
At some disputed barricade,
When Spring comes back with rustling shade
And apple-blossoms fill the air—
I have a rendezvous with Death
When Spring brings back blue days and fair.

    It may be he shall take my hand
And lead me into his dark land
And close my eyes and quench my breath—
It may be I shall pass him still.
I have a rendezvous with Death
On some scarred slope of battered hill,
When Spring comes round again this year
And the first meadow-flowers appear.

    God knows 'twere better to be deep
Pillowed in silk and scented down,
Where Love throbs out in blissful sleep,
Pulse nigh to pulse, and breath to breath,
Where hushed awakenings are dear . . .
But I've a rendezvous with Death
At midnight in some flaming town,
When Spring trips north again this year,
And I to my pledged word am true,
I shall not fail that rendezvous.

A. H. CLOUGH 1819-1861
from
AMOURS DE VOYAGE

Now supposing the French or the Neapolitan soldier
Should by some evil chance come exploring the Maison Serny
(Where the family English are all to assemble for safety),
Am I prepared to lay down my life for the British female?
Really, who knows? One has bowed and talked, till, little by little,
All the natural heat has escaped of the chivalrous spirit.
Oh, one conformed, of course; but one doesn't die for good manners,
Stab or shoot, or be shot, by way of graceful attention.
No, if it should be at all, it should be on the barricades there;
Should I incarnadine ever this inky pacifical finger,
Sooner far should it be for this vapour of Italy's freedom,
Sooner far by the side of the d——d and dirty plebeians.
Ah, for a child in the street I could strike; for the full-blown lady—
Somehow, Eustace, alas! I have not felt the vocation.
Yet these people of course will expect, as of course, my protection,
Vernon in radiant arms stand forth for the lovely Georgina,
And to appear, I suppose, were but common civility. Yes, and
Truly I do not desire they should either be killed or offended.
Oh, and of course, you will say, 'When the time comes, you will
  be ready.'
Ah, but before it comes, am I to presume it will be so?
What I cannot feel now, am I to suppose that I shall feel?
Am I not free to attend for the ripe and indubious instinct?
Am I forbidden to wait for the clear and lawful perception?
Is it the calling of man to surrender his knowledge and insight,
For the mere venture of what may, perhaps, be the virtuous action?
Must we, walking our earth, discern a little, and hoping
Some plain visible task shall yet for our hands be assigned us,—
Must we abandon the future for fear of omitting the present,
Quit our own fireside hopes at the alien call of a neighbour,
To the mere possible shadow of Deity offer the victim?

SIEGFRIED SASSOON b. 1886
DREAMERS

Soldiers are citizens of death's gray land,
    Drawing no dividend from time's tomorrows.
In the great hour of destiny they stand,
    Each with his feuds and jealousies and sorrows.
Soldiers are sworn to action; they must win
    Some flaming fatal climax with their lives.
Soldiers are dreamers; when the guns begin
    They think of firelit homes, clean beds, and wives.

I see them in foul dug-outs, gnawed by rats,
    And in the ruined trenches, lashed with rain,
Dreaming of things they did with balls and bats,
    And mocked by hopeless longing to regain
Bank-holidays, and picture-shows, and spats,
    And going to the office in the train.

A. E. HOUSMAN 1859-1936
THE STREET SOUNDS TO THE SOLDIERS' TREAD

    The street sounds to the soldiers' tread,
        And out we troop to see:
    A single redcoat turns his head,
        He turns and looks at me.

    My man, from sky to sky's so far,
        We never crossed before;
    Such leagues apart the world's ends are,
        We're like to meet no more;

    What thoughts at heart have you and I
        We cannot stop to tell;
    But dead or living, drunk or dry,
        Soldier, I wish you well.

GEORGE MEREDITH 1828-1909
"ATKINS"

Yonder's the man with his life in his hand,
Legs on the march for whatever the land,
  Or to the slaughter, or to the maiming,
  Getting the dole of a dog for pay.
Laurels he clasps in the words "duty done",
England his heart under every sun:—
  Exquisite humour! that gives him a naming
Base to the ear as an ass's bray.

W. H. AUDEN b. 1907

O WHAT IS THAT SOUND WHICH SO THRILLS THE EAR

O what is that sound which so thrills the ear
  Down in the valley drumming, drumming?
Only the scarlet soldiers, dear,
  The soldiers coming.

O what is that light I see flashing so clear
  Over the distance brightly, brightly?
Only the sun on their weapons, dear,
  As they step lightly.

O what are they doing with all that gear,
  What are they doing this morning, this morning?
Only the usual manœuvres, dear,
  Or perhaps a warning.

O why have they left the road down there,
  Why are they suddenly wheeling, wheeling?
Perhaps a change in the orders, dear.
  Why are you kneeling?

O haven't they stopped for the doctor's care,
  Haven't they reined their horses, their horses?
Why, they are none of them wounded, dear,
  None of these forces.

O is it the parson they want with white hair,
  Is it the parson, is it, is it?
No they are passing his gateway, dear,
  Without a visit.

O it must be the farmer who lives so near.
  It must be the farmer so cunning, so cunning?
They have passed the farm already, dear,
  And now they are running.

O where are you going? stay with me here!
  Were the vows you swore deceiving, deceiving?
No, I promised to love you dear,
  But I must be leaving.

O it's broken the lock and splintered the door,
  O it's the gate where they're turning, turning;
Their feet are heavy on the floor
  And their eyes are burning.

A E. HOUSMAN 1859-1936
IN VALLEYS GREEN AND STILL

In valleys green and still
　Where lovers wander maying
They hear from over hill
　A music playing.

Behind the drum and fife,
　Past hawthornwood and hollow,
Through earth and out of life
　The soldiers follow.

The soldier's is the trade:
　In any wind or weather
He steals the heart of maid
　And man together.

The lover and his lass
　Beneath the hawthorn lying
Have heard the soldiers pass,
　And both are sighing.

And down the distance they
　With dying note and swelling
Walk the resounding way
　To the still dwelling.

RUDYARD KIPLING 1865-1936

THE BRIDEGROOM

Call me not false, beloved,
   If, from thy scarce-known breast
So little time removed,
   In other arms I rest.

For this more ancient bride,
   Whom coldly I embrace,
Was constant at my side
   Before I saw thy face.

Our marriage, often set—
   By miracle delayed—
At last is consummate,
   And cannot be unmade.

Live, then, whom Life shall cure,
   Almost, of Memory,
And leave us to endure
   Its immortality.

PAO CHAO d.466 A.D.
Translated from the Chinese by Arthur Waley
THE SCHOLAR RECRUIT

Now late
I follow Time's Necessity:
Mounting a barricade I pacify remote tribes.
Discarding my sash I don a coat of rhinoceros-skin:
Rolling up my skirts I shoulder a black bow.
Even at the very start my strength fails:
What will become of me before it's all over?

THOMAS HARDY 1840-1928

MEN WHO MARCH AWAY

What of the faith and fire within us
    Men who march away
    Ere the barn-cocks say
    Night is growing gray,
Leaving all that here can win us;
What of the faith and fire within us
    Men who march away?

Is it a purblind prank, O think you,
    Friend with the musing eye,
    Who watch us stepping by
    With doubt and dolorous sigh?
Can much pondering so hoodwink you!
Is it a purblind prank, O think you,
    Friend with the musing eye?

Nay. We well see what we are doing,
   Though some may not see—
   Dalliers as they be—
   England's need are we;
Her distress would leave us rueing:
Nay. We well see what we are doing,
   Though some may not see!

In our heart of hearts believing
   Victory crowns the just,
   And that braggarts must
   Surely bite the dust,
Press we to the field ungrieving,
In our heart of hearts believing
   Victory crowns the just.

Hence the faith and fire within us
   Men who march away
   Ere the barn-cocks say
   Night is growing gray,
Leaving all that here can win us;
Hence the faith and fire within us
   Men who march away.

WILFRED SCAWEN BLUNT 1840-1922
GIBRALTAR

Seven weeks of sea, and twice seven days of storm
Upon the huge Atlantic, and once more
We ride into still water and the calm
Of a sweet evening screened by either shore
Of Spain and Barbary. Our toils are o'er,
Our exile is accomplished. Once again
We look on Europe, mistress as of yore
Of the fair earth and of the hearts of men.
Ay, this is the famed rock which Hercules
And Goth and Moor bequeathed us. At this door
England stands sentry. God! to hear the shrill
Sweet treble of her fifes upon the breeze
And at the summons of the rock gun's roar
To see her redcoats marching from the hill!.

C. H. SORLEY 1895-1915
ALL THE HILLS AND VALES ALONG

All the hills and vales along
Earth is bursting into song,
And the singers are the chaps
Who are going to die perhaps.
   O sing, marching men
   Till the valleys ring again.
   Give your gladness to earth's keeping,
   So be glad, when you are sleeping.

Cast away regret and rue,
Think what you are marching to.
Little live, great pass.
Jesus Christ and Barabbas

Were found the same day.
This died, that went his way.
  So sing with joyful breath,
  For why, you are going to death.
  Teeming earth will surely store
  All the gladness that you pour.

Earth that never doubts nor fears,
Earth that knows of death, not tears,
Earth that bore with joyful ease
Hemlock for Socrates,
Earth that blossomed and was glad
'Neath the cross that Christ had,
Shall rejoice and blossom too
When the bullet reaches you.
  Wherefore, men marching
  On the road to death, sing!
  Pour your gladness on earth's head,
  So be merry, so be dead.

From the hills and valleys earth
Shouts back the sound of mirth,
Tramp of feet and lilt of song
Ringing all the road along.
All the music of their going,
Ringing, swinging glad song-throwing,
Earth will echo still when foot
Lies numb and voice mute.
  On, marching men, on
  To the gates of death with song.
  Sow your gladness for earth's reaping,
  So you may be glad, though sleeping.
  Strew your gladness on earth's bed.
  So be merry, so be dead.

HERMAN MELVILLE 1819-1891

BALL'S BLUFF
A Reverie
October 1861

One noonday, at my window in the town,
    I saw a sight—saddest that eyes can see—
    Young soldiers marching lustily
        Unto the wars,
With fifes, and flags in mottoed pageantry;
    While all the porches, walks, and doors
Were rich with ladies cheering royally.

They moved like Juny morning on the wave,
    Their hearts were fresh as clover in its prime
    (It was the breezy summer-time),
        Life throbbed so strong,
How should they dream that Death in a rosy clime
    Would come to thin their shining throng?
Youth feels immortal, like the gods sublime.

Weeks passed; and at my window, leaving bed,
    By night I mused, of easeful sleep bereft,
    On those brave boys (Ah War! thy theft);
        Some marching feet
Found pause at last by cliffs Potomac cleft;
    Wakeful I mused, while in the street
Far footfalls died away till none were left.

SHEILA SHANNON b. 1913

SOLDIER AND GIRL SLEEPING

(On a painting by William Scott)

It is late, already, it is night;
But still they wait still spin the moments out:
There is time yet and they rest
Side by side on the hard station bench:
For the train will come, will break
These two apart and bear the half way.

Parting in love is not so hard a thing,
(Leaving within a crystal certitude
Wrapping within the pain a kernel joy),
As parting in love's echo;
For outgoing love bears on its ebbing tide
All things away and is more sure
In its finality than Death.

These two are sleeping now.
She sleeps so lightly
Wavering on the further verge of waking;
But his stillness holds her firm
In the fixed circle of his dream;
She lies within the cavities of his being
The bright imagination of his heart
And through his darkened eyes sees not
The falling hand of Time,
Nor through his sleeping ears can hear
The tiger trains prowl in and out.

They sleep:
And parting has no time for them
Nor place to hurt them in.

URSULA WOOD b.1911
PENELOPE

Certain parting does not wait its hour
for separation; too soon the shadow lies
upon the heart and chokes the voice, its power
drives on the minutes, it implies
tomorrow while today's still here.

They sat by firelight and his shadow fell
for the last time, she thought, black patterning gold
sharp on the firelit wall.   So, to compel
the evening to outlast the morning's cold
dawn by the quayside and the unshed tears,

she took a charred twig from the hearth and drew
the outline of his shadow on the wall.
"These were his features, this the hand I knew."
She heard her voice saying the words through all
the future days of solitude and fear.

JOHN CLARE 1793-1864
THE SOLDIER

Home furthest off grows dearer from the way;
And when the army in the Indias lay
Friends' letters coming from his native place
Were like old neighbours with their country face.
And every opportunity that came
Opened the sheet to gaze upon the name
Of that loved village where he left his sheep
For more contented peaceful folk to keep;
And friendly faces absent many a year
Would from such letters in his mind appear.
And when his pockets, chafing through the case,
Wore it quite out ere others took the place,
Right loath to be of company bereft
He kept the fragments while a bit was left.

III

WILLIAM MORRIS 1834-1896
THE JUDGMENT OF GOD[1]
"Swerve to the left, son Roger," he said,
  "When you catch his eyes through the helmet-slit,
Swerve to the left, then out at his head,
  And the Lord God give you joy of it!"

The blue owls on my father's hood
  Were a little dimm'd as I turned away;
This giving up of blood for blood
  Will finish here somehow to-day.

So — when I walk'd out from the tent,
  Their howling almost blinded me;
Yet for all that I was not bent
  By any shame. Hard by, the sea

Made a noise like the aspens where
  We did that wrong, but now the place
Is very pleasant, and the air
  Blows cool on any passer's face.

And all the wrong is gather'd now
  Into the circle of these lists—
Yea, howl out, butchers! tell me how
  His hands were cut off at the wrists;

And how Lord Roger bore his face
  A league above his spear-point, high
Above the owls, to that strong place
  Among the waters — yea, yea, cry:

"What a brave champion we have got!
   Sir Oliver, the flower of all
The Hainault knights." The day being hot,
   He sat beneath a broad white pall,

White linen over all his steel;
   What a good knight he look'd! his sword
Laid thwart his knees; he liked to feel
   Its steadfast edge clear as his word.

And he look'd solemn; how his love
   Smiled whitely on him sick with fear!
How all the ladies up above
   Twisted their pretty hands! so near

The fighting was — Ellayne! Ellayne!
   They cannot love like you can, who
Would burn your hands off, if that pain
   Could win a kiss — am I not true

To you for ever? therefore I
   Do not fear death nor anything;
If I should limp home wounded, why,
   While I lay sick you would but sing,

And soothe me into quiet sleep.
   If they spat on the recreaunt knight,
Threw stones at him, and cursed him deep,
   Why then — what then; your hand would light

So gently on his drawn-up face,
   And you would kiss him, and in soft
Cool scented clothes would lap him, pace
   The quiet room and weep oft, — oft

Would turn and smile, and brush his cheek
   With your sweet chin and mouth; and in
The order'd garden you would seek
   The biggest roses — any sin.

And these say: "No more now my knight,
   Or God's knight any longer" — you
Being than they so much more white,
   So much more pure and good and true,

Will cling to me for ever — there,
   Is not that wrong turn'd right at last
Through all these years, and I wash'd clean?
   Say, yea, Ellayne; the time is past,

Since on that Christmas-day last year
   Up to your feet the fire crept,
And the smoke through the brown leaves sere
   Blinded your dear eyes that you wept;

Was it not I that caught you then,
   And kissed you on the saddle-bow?
Did not the blue owl mark the men
   Whose spears stood like the corn a-row?

This Oliver is a right good knight,
   And must needs beat me, as I fear,
Unless I catch him in the fight,
   My father's crafty way — John, here!

Bring up the men from the south gate,
   To help me if I fall or win,
For even if I beat, their hate
   Will grow to more than this mere grin.

ROBERT FROST b. 1875

RANGE-FINDING

The battle rent a cobweb diamond-strung
And cut a flower beside a ground bird's nest
Before it stained a single human breast.
The stricken flower bent double and so hung.
And still the bird revisited her young.
A butterfly its fall had dispossessed
A moment sought in air his flower of rest,
Then lightly stooped to it and fluttering clung.

On the bare upland pasture there had spread
O'er night 'twixt mullein stalks a wheel of thread
And straining cables wet with silver dew.
A sudden passing bullet shook it dry.
The indwelling spider ran to greet the fly,
But finding nothing, sullenly withdrew.

C. DAY LEWIS b. 1904

THE STAND-TO

Autumn met me to-day as I walked over Castle Hill.
The wind that had set our corn by the ears was blowing still:
Autumn, who takes the leaves and the long days, crisped the air
With a tang of action, a taste of death; and the wind blew fair

From the east for men and barges massed on the other side—
Men maddened by numbers or stolid by nature, they have their pride
As we in work or children, but now a contracting will
Crumples their meek petitions and holds them poised to kill.

Last night a Stand-To was ordered. Thirty men of us here
Came out to guard the starlit village — my men who wear
Unwitting the season's beauty, the received truth of the spade—
Roadmen, farm labourers, masons, turned to another trade.

A dog barked over the fields, the candle stars put a sheen
On the rifles ready, the sandbags shrouded with evergreen:
The dawn wind blew, the stars winked out on the posts where we lay,
The order came, Stand Down, and thirty went away.

Since a cold wind from Europe blows the words back in my teeth,
Since autumn shortens the days and the odds against our death,
And the harvest moon is waxing and high tides threaten harm,
Since last night may be the last night all thirty men go home,

I write this verse to record the men who have watched with me—
Spot who is good at darts, Squibby at repartee,
Mark and Cyril, the dead shots, Ralph with a ploughman's gait,
Gibson, Harris and Long, old hands for the barricade.

Whiller the lorry-driver, Francis and Rattlesnake,
Fred and Charles and Stan — these nights I have lain awake
And thought of my thirty men and the autumn wind that blows
The apples down too early and shatters the autumn rose.

Destiny, History, Duty, Fortitude, Honour — all
The words of the politicians seem too big or too small
For the ragtag fighters of lane and shadow, the love that has grown
Familiar as working-clothes, faithful as bone to bone.

Blow, autumn wind, upon orchard and rose! Blow leaves along
Our lanes, but sing through me for the lives that are worth a sing!
Narrowing days have darkened the vistas that hurt my eyes,
But pinned to the heart of darkness a tattered fire-flag flies.

WILLIAM WORDSWORTH 1770-1850

THE FRENCH AND SPANISH GUERRILLAS

Hunger, and sultry heat, and nipping blast
From bleak hill-top, and length of march by night
Through heavy swamp, or over snow-clad height—
These hardships ill-sustained, these dangers past,
The roving Spanish Bands are reached at last,
Charged, and dispersed like foam: but as a flight
Of scattered quails by signs do reunite,
So these,—and, heard of once again, are chased
With combinations of long practised art
And newly kindled hope; but they are fled—
Gone are they, viewless as the buried dead:
Where now? — Their sword is at the Foeman's heart!
And thus from year to year his walk they thwart,
And hang like dreams around his guilty bed.

FREDERIC PROKOSCH b. 1909
THE CAMPAIGN

The snow falls silently through the unnatural forest,
Falls silently over the frozen brow and frozen hand.
They are terribly sleepy. But still their hard bodies
Move on and on and on over the frozen land.

They do not hear the rustle of certain forgotten moments,
The lamplight falling through the rain on the pear tree and the pears.
The bells on a Sunday morning, and the sweet, solemn faces,
The sudden joy on a girl's face as she leans over the stairs:

They do not quite recall, for even then they did not notice,
That something precious had gone away, had quietly gone away;
The hand had grown unsteady; the love had lost its pleasure,
And the low call of beasts disturbed the calm summer's day.

They cannot possibly hear the ruddy approach of evening,
Or the horses and the naked horsemen approaching the stream.
Snow falls, and they cannot hear the tinkling teacup
Take on the oracular magnitude and anguish of a dream.

They pause. And now they fall asleep. A strange new power
Governs their lives, redistributing the happiness and the pain
And the nameless longings which gave their lives a secret pattern.
Their destinies flow on and on over the frozen plain

Like waves over the sea. They sought, in this career of killing,
Escape from the hushed and paralysed career of the plants.
Snow falls, and the leaning bayonets are glimmering
In the firelight. They sleep. None hear the soft advance

Through the treacherous mask of the birches: the polar twilight
Has washed away the necessity for belief or disbelief.
These soldiers do not hear, winding stealthily through the forest
The savage and irresistible footfalls of their grief.

A. H. CLOUGH 1819-1861

from

AMOURS DE VOYAGE

Yes, we are fighting at last, it appears. This morning as usual,
Murray, as usual, in hand, I enter the Caffè Nuovo;
Seating myself with a sense as it were of a change in the weather,
Not understanding, however, but thinking mostly of Murray,
And, for to-day is their day, of the Campidoglio Marbles;
Caffè-latte! I call to the waiter, — and *Non c' è latte*,
This is the answer he makes me, and this is the sign of a battle.
So I sit; and truly they seem to think anyone else more
Worthy than me of attention. I wait for my milkless *nero*,
Free to observe undistracted all sorts and sizes of persons,
Blending civilian and soldier in strangest costume, coming in, and
Gulping in hottest haste, still standing, their coffee, — withdrawing
Eagerly, jangling a sword on the steps, or jogging a musket
Slung to the shoulder behind. They are fewer, moreover, than usual,
Much and silenter far; and so I begin to imagine
Something is really afloat. Ere I leave, the Caffè is empty,
Empty too the streets, in all its length the Corso
Empty, and empty I see to my right and left the Condotti.
 Twelve o'clock, on the Pincian Hill, with lots of English,
Germans, Americans, French,—the Frenchmen, too, are protected,—
So we stand in the sun, but afraid of a probable shower;
So we stand and stare, and see, to the left of St. Peter's,
Smoke, from the cannon, white,—but that is at intervals only,—
Black, from a burning house, we suppose, by the Cavalleggieri;
And we believe we discern some lines of men descending
Down through the vineyard-slopes, and catch a bayonet gleaming.
Every ten minutes, however,—in this there is no misconception,—
Comes a great white puff from behind Michel Angelo's dome, and
After a space the report of a real big gun,—not the Frenchman's!—
That must be doing some work. And so we watch and conjecture.
 Shortly, an Englishman comes, who says he has been to St. Peter's,
Seen the Piazza and troops, but that is all he can tell us;
So we watch and sit, and, indeed, it begins to be tiresome.—

All this smoke is outside; when it has come to the inside,
It will be time, perhaps, to descend and retreat to our houses.
    Half-past one, or two. The report of small arms frequent,
Sharp and savage indeed; that cannot all be for nothing:
So we watch and wonder; but guessing is tiresome, very.
Weary of wondering, watching, and guessing, and gossiping idly,
Down I go, and pass through the quiet streets with the knots of
National Guards patrolling, and flags hanging out at the windows,
English, American, Danish,—and, after offering to help an
Irish family moving *en masse* to the Maison Serny,
After endeavouring idly to minister balm to the trembling
Quinquagenarian fears of two lone British spinsters,
Go to make sure of my dinner before the enemy enter.
But by this there are signs of stragglers returning; and voices
Talk, though you don't believe it, of guns and prisoners taken;
And on the walls you read the first bulletin of the morning.—
This is all that I saw, and all I know of the battle.

ANONYMOUS C.124 B.C.

Translated from the Chinese by Arthur Waley

FIGHTING SOUTH OF THE CASTLE

They fought south of the Castle,
They died north of the wall.
They died in the moors and were not buried.
Their flesh was the food of crows.
"Tell the crows we are not afraid;
We have died in the moors and cannot be buried
Crows, how can our bodies escape you?"
The waters flowed deep
And the rushes in the pool were dark.
The riders fought and were slain:
Their horses wander neighing.

By the bridge there was a house.
Was it south, was it north?
The harvest was never gathered.
How can we give you your offerings?
You served your Prince faithfully,
Though all in vain.
I think of you, faithful soldiers;
Your service shall not be forgotten.
For in the morning you went out to battle
And at night you did not return.

JAMES ELROY FLECKER 1884-1915
TAOPING

Across the vast blue-shadow-sweeping plain
The gathered armies darken through the grain,
Swinging curved swords and dragon-sculptured spears,
Footmen, and tiger-hearted cavaliers.
Their Government (whose fragrance Poets sing)
Hath bidden break the rebels of Taoping,
And fire and fell the monstrous fort of fools
Who dream that men may dare the deathless rules.
Such, grim example even now can show
Where high above the Van, in triple row,
First fiery blossom of rebellion's tree,
Twelve spear-stemmed heads are dripping silently.
(On evil day you sought, O ashen lips,
The kiss of women from our town of ships,
Nor ever dreamt, O spies, of falser spies,
The poppied cup and passion-mocking eyes!)

By these grim civil trophies undismayed,
In lacquered panoplies the chiefs parade.
Behind, the plain's floor rocks: the armies come:
The rose-round lips blow battles horns: the drum
Booms oriental measure.   Earth exults.

And still behind, the tottering catapults
Pulled by slow slaves, grey backs with crimson lines,
Roll resolutely west. And still behind,
Down the canal's hibiscus-shaded marge
The glossy mules draw on the cedar barge,
Railed silver, blue-silk-curtained, which within
Bears the Commander, the old Mandarin,
Who never left his palace gates before,
But hath grown blind reading great books of war.

Now level on the land and cloudless red
The sun's slow circle dips toward the dead
Night-hunted, all the monstrous flags are furled:
The Armies halt, and round them halts the World.
A phantom wind flies out among the rice;
Hush turns the twin horizons in her vice;
Air thickens: earth is pressed upon earth's core.
The cedar barge swings gently to the shore
Among her silver shadows and the swans:
The blind old man sets down his pipe of bronze.
The long whips cease. The slaves slacken the chain.
The gaunt-towered engines space the silent plain.
The hosts like men held in a frozen dream
Stiffen. The breastplates drink the scarlet gleam.
But the Twelve Heads with shining sockets stare
Further and further West. Have they seen there,
Black on blood's sea and huger than Death's wing,
Their *cannon-bowelled* fortress of Taoping?

THOMAS LOVE PEACOCK 1785-1866

THE WAR SONG OF DINAS VAWR

The mountain sheep are sweeter,
But the valley sheep are fatter;
We therefore deemed it meeter
To carry off the latter.
We made an expedition;
We met an host, and quelled it;
We forced a strong position,
And killed the men who held it.

On Dyfed's richest valley,
Where herds of kine were browsing,
We made a mighty sally,
To furnish our carousing.
Fierce warriors rushed to meet us;
We met them, and o'erthrew them:
They struggled hard to beat us;
But we conquered them, and slew them.

As we drove our prize at leisure,
The King marched forth to catch us:
His rage surpassed all measure,
But his people could not match us.
He fled to his hall-pillars;
And, ere our force we led off,
Some sacked his house and cellars,
While others cut his head off.

We there, in strife bewildering,
Spilt blood enough to swim in:
We orphaned many children,
And widowed many women.
The eagles and the ravens
We glutted with our foemen;
The heroes and the cravens,
The spearmen and the bowmen.

We brought away from battle,
And much their land bemoaned them,
Two thousand head of cattle,
And the head of him who owned them:
Ednyfed, King of Dyfed,
His head was borne before us;
His wine and beasts supplied our feasts,
And his overthrow, our chorus

HERMAN MELVILLE 1819-1891

SHILOH

A Requiem, April, 1862

Skimming lightly, wheeling still,
　　The swallows fly low
Over the field in clouded days,
　　The forest-field of Shiloh—
Over the field where April rain
Solaced the parched one stretched in pain
Through the pause of night
That followed the Sunday fight
　　Around the church of Shiloh—
The church so lone, the log-built one,
That echoed to many a parting groan
　　　　And natural prayer
　　Of dying foemen mingled there—
Foemen at morn, but friends at eve—
　　Fame or country least their care:
(What like a bullet can undeceive!)
　　But now they lie low,
While over them the swallows skim
　　And all is hushed at Shiloh.

LIONEL JOHNSON 1867-1902

CHILD OF WAR

Her ivory face, quivering but trembling not,
Upheld against a sky of angry storm;
She stands upon her savage chariot,
Fronting the field of Death, a silent form.
The eagle's daughter, this day she forgot
Pity and peace for the first time, and went
To watch the waves of war break, and be spent.

Homeward, with shadows passing on her face,
Strange lights with strange tears battling in her eyes;
She goes the triumph way of her old race,
Watching the eagles gather in the skies.
Tasted hath she this day death's busy place:
And in her heart called up to equal fight,
Daughter of eagles, loathing and delight.

WILLIAM MORRIS 1834-1896

THE KNIGHT IN PRISON

Wearily, drearily,
Half the day long,
Flap the great banners
High over the stone;
Strangely and eerily
Sounds the wind's song,
Bending the banner-poles.

While, all alone,
Watching the loophole's spark,
Lie I, with life all dark,
Feet tethered, hands fetter'd
Fast to the stone,
The grim walls square letter'd
With prison'd men's groan.

Still strain the banner-poles
Through the wind's song,
Westward the banner rolls
Over my wrong.

IV

ALICE MEYNELL 1847-1922

SUMMER IN ENGLAND 1914

On London fell a clearer light;
   Caressing pencils of the sun
Defined the distances, the white
   Houses transfigured one by one,
The "long, unlovely street" impearled.
O what a sky has walked the world!

Most happy year! And out of town
   The hay was prosperous, and the wheat;
The silken harvest climbed the down;
   Moon after moon was heavenly-sweet
Stroking the bread within the sheaves,
Looking twixt apples and their leaves.

And while this rose made round her cup,
   The armies died convulsed. And when
This chaste young silver sun went up
   Softly, a thousand shattered men,
One wet corruption, heaped the plain
After a league-long throb of pain.

Flower following tender flower; and birds,
   And berries; and benignant skies
Made thrive the serried flocks and herds.—
   Yonder are men shot through the eyes.
     Love, hide thy face
From man's unpardonable race!

WILFRED OWEN 1893-1918

THE SENTRY

We'd found an old Boche dug-out, and he knew,
And gave us hell, for shell on frantic shell
Hammered on top, but never quite burst through.
Rain guttering down in waterfalls of slime
Kept slush waist-high that, rising hour by hour,
Choked up the steps too thick with clay to climb.
What murk of air remained stank old, and sour
With fumes of whizz-bangs, and the smell of men
Who'd lived there years, and left their curse in the den,
If not their corpses . . .

                    There we herded from the blast
Of whizz-bangs, but one found our door at last,—
Buffeting eyes and breath, snuffing the candles.
And thud! flump! thud! down the steep steps came thumping
And splashing in the flood, deluging muck—
The sentry's body; then, his rifle, handles
Of old Boche bombs, and mud in ruck on ruck.
We dredged him up, for killed, until he whined
"O, sir, my eyes — I'm blind — I'm blind, I'm blind!"
Coaxing I held a flame against his lids
And said if he could see the least blurred light
He was not blind; in time he'd get all right.
"I can't," he sobbed.   Eyeballs, huge-bulged like squids',
Watch my dreams still; but I forgot him there
In posting next for duty, and sending a scout
To beg a stretcher somewhere, and floundering about
To other posts under the shrieking air.

        .   .   .   .   .   .

Those other wretches, how they bled and spewed,
And one who would have drowned himself for good,—
I try not to remember these things now.
Let dread hark back for one word only: how
Half listening to that sentry's moans and jumps,

And the wild chattering of his broken teeth,
Renewed most horribly whenever crumps
Pummelled the roof and slogged the air beneath—
Through the dense din, I say, we heard him shout
"I see your lights!" But ours had long died out.

SIEGFRIED SASSOON b. 1886

DOES IT MATTER

Does it matter?—losing your legs? . . .
For people will always be kind,
And you need not show that you mind
When the others come in after football
To gobble their muffins and eggs.

Does it matter?—losing your sight? . . .
There's such splendid work for the blind;
And people will always be kind,
As you sit on the terrace remembering
And turning your face to the light.

Do they matter? — those dreams from the pit? . . .
You can drink and forget and be glad,
And people won't say that you're mad
For they'll know that you've fought for your country
And no one will worry a bit.

THOMAS HOOD 1799-1845
FAITHLESS NELLIE GRAY

Ben Battle was a soldier bold,
    And used to war's alarms;
But a cannon-ball took off his legs,
    So he laid down his arms.

Now as they bore him off the field,
    Said he, 'Let others shoot,
For here I leave my second leg,
    And the forty-second Foot!'

The army-surgeons made him limbs;
    Said he:—'They're only pegs:
But there's as wooden members quite
    As represent my legs!'

Now Ben he loved a pretty maid,
    Her name was Nellie Gray:
So he went to pay her his devours
    When he'd devoured his pay!

But when he called on Nellie Gray,
    She made him quite a scoff;
And when she saw his wooden legs
    Began to take them off!

'O, Nellie Gray! O, Nellie Gray!
    Is this your love so warm?
The love that loves a scarlet coat
    Should be more uniform!'

She said, 'I loved a soldier once,
    For he was blythe and brave;
But I will never have a man
    With both legs in the grave!

'Before you had those timber toes,
　　Your love I did allow,
But then, you know, you stand upon
　　Another footing now!'

'O, Nellie Gray! O, Nellie Gray!
　　For all your jeering speeches,
At duty's call, I left my legs,
　　In Badajos's *breaches*!'

'Why then,' she said, 'you've lost the feet
　　Of legs in war's alarms,
And now you cannot wear your shoes
　　Upon your feats of arms!'

'Oh, false and fickle Nellie Gray;
　　I know why you refuse:—
Though I've no feet some other man
　　Is standing in my shoes!

'I wish I ne'er had seen your face;
　　But now, a long farewell!
For you will be my death, alas!
　　You will not be my *Nell*!'

Now when he went from Nellie Gray,
　　His heart so heavy got—
And life was such a burden grown,
　　It made him take a knot!

So round his melancholy neck,
　　A rope he did entwine,
And, for his second time in life,
　　Enlisted in the Line!

One end he tied around a beam,
　　And then removed his pegs,

45

And as his legs were off, — of course,
    He soon was off his legs!

And there he hung until he was dead
    As any nail in town,—
For though distress had cut him up,
    It could not cut him down!

A dozen men sat on his corpse
    To find out why he died—
And they buried Ben in four cross-roads
    With a stake in his inside!

THOMAS HARDY 1840-1928

THE MAN HE KILLED

"Had he and I but met
    By some old ancient Inn,
We should have sat us down to wet
    Right many a nipperkin!

"But ranged as infantry
    And staring face to face,
I shot at him as he at me,
    And killed him in his place.

"I shot him dead because—
    Because he was my foe,
Just so: my foe of course he was;
    That's clear enough; although

"He thought he'd list, perhaps,
    Offhand like — Just as I—
Was out of work — had sold his traps—
    No other reason why.

"Yes; quaint and curious war is!
    You shoot a fellow down
You'd treat if met where any bar is,
    Or help to half-a-crown."

ROY CAMPBELL b. 1902
HIALMAR

The firing ceased and like a wounded foe
The day bled out in crimson: wild and high
A far hyena sent his voice of woe
Tingling in faint hysteria through the sky.

Thick lay the fatal harvest of the fight
In the grey twilight when the newly dead
Collect those brindled scavengers of night
Whose bloodshot eyes must candle them to bed.

The dead slept on: but one among them rose
Out of his trance, and turned a patient eye
To where like cankers in a burning rose,
Out of the fading scarlet of the sky,

Great birds, descending, settled on the stones:
He knew their errand and he knew how soon
The wolf must make a pulpit of their bones
To skirl his shrill hosannas to the moon.

Great adjutants came wheeling from the hills,
And chaplain crows with smug, self-righteous face,

And vultures bald and red about the gills
As any hearty colonel at the base.

All creatures that grow fat on beauty's wreck,
They ranged themselves expectant round the kill,
And like a shrivelled arm each raw, red neck
Lifted the rusty dagger of its bill.

Thus to the largest of that bony tribe
'O merry bird,' he shouted, 'work your will,
I offer my clean body as a bribe
That when upon its flesh you've gorged your fill,

'You'll take my heart and bear it in your beak
To where my sweetheart combs her yellow hair
Beside the Vaal: and if she bids you speak
Tell her you come to represent me there.

'Flounce out your feathers in their sleekest trim,
Affect the brooding softness of the dove—
Yea, smile, thou skeleton so foul and grim,
As fits the bland ambassador of love!

'And tell her, when the nights are wearing late
And the grey moonlight smoulders on her hair,
To brood no more upon her ghostly mate
Nor on the phantom children she would bear.

'Tell her I fought as blindly as the rest,
That none of them had wronged me whom I killed,
And she may seek within some other breast
The promise that I leave her unfulfilled.

'I should have been too tired for love or mirth
Stung as I am, and sickened by the truth—
Old men have hunted beauty from the earth
Over the broken bodies of our youth!'

ALUN LEWIS 1920-1944
AFTER DUNKIRK

I have been silent a lifetime
As a stabbed man,
And stolid, showing nothing
As a refugee.
But inwardly I have wept.
The blood has flown inwardly into the spirit
Through the gaping wound of the world.
And only the little worm,
The small white tapeworm of the soul,
Lived on unknown within my blood.

But now I have this boon, to speak again,
I have no more desire to express
The old relationships, of love fulfilled
Or stultified, capacity for pain,
Nor to say gracefully all that the poets have said
Of one or other of the old compulsions.
For now the times are gathered for confession.

First, then, remember Faith
Haggard with thoughts that complicate
What statesmen's speeches try to simplify;
Horror of war, the ear half-catching
Rumours of rape in crumbling towns;
Love of mankind, impelling men
To murder and to mutilate; and then
Despair of man that nurtures self-contempt
And makes men toss their careless lives away,
While joy becomes an idiot's grin
Fixed in a shaving mirror in whose glass
The brittle systems of the world revolve.

And next, the rough immediate life of camp
And barracks where the phallic bugle rules
The regimented orchestra of love;

The subterfuges of democracy, the stench
Of breath in crowded tents, the grousing queues,
And bawdy songs incessantly resung
And dull relaxing in the dirty bar;
The difficult tolerance of all that is
Mere rigid brute routine; the odd
Sardonic scorn of desolate self-pity,
The pathetic contempt of the lonely for the crowd;
And, as the crystal slowly forms,
A growing self-detachment making man
Less home-sick, fearful, proud,
But less a man.
Beneath all this
The dark imagination that would pierce
Infinite night and reach the waiting arms
And soothe the guessed-at tears.

And then the final change.   For discipline
Becomes a test of self; one learns to bear
Insult as quietly as if it were
A physical deformity.   But hope
Has left the calm humanity that waits
In silence for the zero hour.
That first great ordeal over,
New resolution grows
In shell-shocked minds of frightened boys
To live again, within the heightened vision
Of life as they saw it in the hour of battle
When the worn and beautiful faces of the half-forgotten
Came softly round them with the holy power
To raise the wounded and the dying succour,
Making complete all that was misbegotten
Or clumsily abused or left neglected.

And as the burning town falls down the wake
And white waves spread their fans and day grows bright,
Then sea and sky and wheeling gulls commingle
In the smiles of dying children and the joy
Of luckier babies playing in the cot.

WALTER DE LA MARE b. 1873
KEEP INNOCENCY

Like an old battle, youth is wild
With bugle and spear, and counter cry,
Fanfare and drummery, yet a child
Dreaming of that sweet chivalry,
The piercing terror cannot see.

He, with a mild and serious eye,
Along the azure of the years,
Sees the sweet pomp sweep hurtling by;
But he sees not death's blood and tears,
Sees not the plunging of the spears.

And all the strident horror of
Horse and rider, in red defeat,
Is only music fine enough
To lull him into slumber sweet
In fields where ewe and lambkin bleat.

O, if with such simplicity
Himself take arms and suffer war;
With beams his targe shall gilded be,
Though in the thickening gloom be far
The steadfast light of any star!

Though hoarse War's eagle on him perch,
Quickened with guilty lightnings — there
It shall in vain for terror search,
Where a child's eyes 'neath bloody hair
Gaze purely through the dingy air.

And when the wheeling rout is spent,
Though in the heaps of slain he lie;
Or lonely in his last content;
Quenchless shall burn in secrecy
The flame Death knows his victors by.

PATRIC DICKINSON b. 1914

WAR

Cold are the stones
That built the wall of Troy;
Cold are the bones
Of the dead Greek boy

Who for some vague thought
Of honour fell,
Nor why he fought
Could clearly tell.

Innocence hired to kill
Lies pitilessly dead.
Stone and bone lie still.
Helen turns in bed.

STEPHEN SPENDER b. 1909

ULTIMA RATIO REGUM

The guns spell money's ultimate reason
In letters of lead on the spring hillside.
But the boy lying dead under the olive trees
Was too young and too silly
To have been notable to their important eye.
He was a better target for a kiss.

When he lived, tall factory hooters never summoned him.
Nor did restaurant plate-glass doors revolve to wave him in.
His name never appeared in the papers.
The world maintained its traditional wall
Round the dead with their gold sunk deep as a well,
While his life, intangible as a Stock Exchange rumour, drifted outside.

O too lightly he threw down his cap
One day when the breeze threw petals from the trees.
The unflowering wall sprouted with guns,
Machine-gun anger quickly scythed the grasses;
Flags and leaves fell from hands and branches;
The tweed cap rotted in the nettles.

Consider his life which was valueless
In terms of employment, hotel ledgers, news files.
Consider.   One bullet in ten thousand kills a man.
Ask.   Was so much expenditure justified
On the death of one so young and so silly
Lying under the olive trees, O world, O death?

ROBERT SOUTHEY 1774-1843

THE BATTLE OF BLENHEIM

It was a summer evening,
   Old Kaspar's work was done,
And he before his cottage door
   Was sitting in the sun,
And by him sported on the green
His little grandchild Wilhelmine.

She saw her brother Peterkin
   Roll something large and round,
Which he beside the rivulet
   In playing there had found;
He came to ask what he had found,
That was so large, and smooth, and round.

Old Kaspar took it from the boy,
   Who stood expectant by;
And then the old man shook his head,
   And, with a natural sigh,
"'Tis some poor fellow's skull," said he,
"Who fell in the great victory.

"I find them in the garden,
   For there's many here about;
And often when I go to plough,
   The ploughshare turns them out!
For many thousand men," said he,
"Were slain in that great victory."

"Now tell us what 'twas all about,"
   Young Peterkin, he cries;
And little Wilhelmine looks up
   With wonder-waiting eyes;
"Now tell us all about the war,
And what they fought each other for."

"It was the English," Kaspar cried,
   "Who put the French to rout;
But what they fought each other for,
   I could not well make out;
But everybody said," quoth he,
"That 'twas a famous victory.

"My father lived at Blenheim then,
   Yon little stream hard by;
They burnt his dwelling to the ground,
   And he was forced to fly;
So with his wife and child he fled,
Nor had he where to rest his head.

"With fire and sword the country round
   Was wasted far and wide,
And many a childing mother then,

And new-born baby died;
But things like that, you know, must be
At every famous victory.

"They say it was a shocking sight
 After the field was won;
For many thousand bodies here
 Lay rotting in the sun;
But things like that, you know, must be
After a famous victory.

"Great praise the Duke of Marlbro' won,
 And our good Prince Eugene."
"Why 'twas a very wicked thing!"
 Said little Wilhelmine.
"Nay . . nay . . my little girl," quoth he,
"It was a famous victory.

"And every body praised the Duke
 Who this great fight did win."
"But what good came of it at last?"
 Quoth little Peterkin.
"Why that I cannot tell," said he,
"But 'twas a famous victory."

V

WALLACE STEVENS b. 1879

THE DEATH OF A SOLDIER

Life contracts and death is expected,
As in a season of autumn
The soldier falls.

He does not become a three days personage,
Imposing his separation,
Calling for pomp.

Death is absolute and without memorial,
As in a season of autumn,
When the wind stops,

When the wind stops and, over the heavens,
The clouds go, nevertheless,
In their direction.

ERNEST RHYS b. 1859

LOST IN FRANCE

He had the plowman's strength
In the grasp of his hand.
He could see a crow
Three miles away,
And the trout beneath the stone.
He could hear the green oats growing,
And the sou'-west making rain;
And the wheel upon the hill
When it left the level road.
He could make a gate, and dig a pit,
And plow as straight as stone can fall.
And he is dead.

EDWARD THOMAS 1878-1917

A PRIVATE

This ploughman dead in battle slept out of doors
Many a frozen night, and merrily
Answered staid drinkers, good bedmen, and all bores:
'At Mrs. Greenland's Hawthorn Bush,' said he,
'I slept.' None knew which bush. Above the town,
Beyond "The Drover," a hundred spot the down
In Wiltshire. And where now at last he sleeps
More sound in France — that, too, he secret keeps.

EDWARD THOMAS 1878-1917

IN MEMORIAM

Easter 1915

The flowers left thick at nightfall in the wood
This Eastertide call into mind the men,
Now far from home, who, with their sweethearts, should
Have gathered them and will do never again.

ROBERT FROST b. 1875

A SOLDIER

He is that fallen lance that lies as hurled,
That lies unlifted now, come dew, come rust,
But still lies pointed as it ploughed the dust.
If we who sight along it round the world,
See nothing worthy to have been its mark,
It is because like men we look too near,
Forgetting that as fitted to the sphere,
Our missiles always make too short an arc.
They fall, they rip the grass, they intersect
The curve of earth, and striking break their own;
They make us cringe for metal-point on stone.
But this we know, the obstacle that checked
And tripped the body, shot the spirit on
Further than target ever showed or shone.

WALT WHITMAN 1819-1892
A SIGHT IN CAMP

A sight in camp in the daybreak grey and dim,
As from my tent I emerge so early sleepless,
As slow I walk in the cool fresh air the path near by the hospital tent,
Three forms I see on stretchers lying, brought out there untended lying,
Over each a blanket spread, ample brownish woollen blanket,
Grey and heavy blanket, folding, covering all.

Curious I halt and silent stand,
There with light fingers I from the face of the nearest, the first
    just lift the blanket;
Who are you, elderly man so gaunt and grim with well-gray'd
    hair, and flesh all sunken about the eyes?
Who are you my dear comrade?

Then to the second I step — and who are you my child and darling?
Who are you, sweet boy with cheeks yet blooming?

Then to the third — a face nor child nor old, very calm, as of
    beautiful yellow-white ivory:
Young man I think I know you — I think this face is the face
    of the Christ Himself,
Dead and divine and brother of all, and here again He lies.

HERMAN MELVILLE 1819-1891
ON THE HOME GUARDS
Who perished in the defence of Lexington, Missouri

  The men who here in harness died
    Fell not in vain, though in defeat.
  They by their end well fortified
    The Cause, and built retreat
  (With memory of their valour tried)
  For emulous hearts in many an after fray—
  Hearts sore beset, which died at bay.

JOHN MCCRAE

IN FLANDERS FIELDS

In Flanders fields the poppies blow
Between the crosses, row on row,
   That mark our place; and in the sky
   The larks, still bravely singing, fly
Scarce heard amid the guns below.

We are the dead. Short days ago
We lived, felt dawn, saw sunset glow,
   Loved and were loved, and now we lie
      In Flanders fields.

Take up our quarrel with the foe:
To you from failing hands we throw
   The torch; be yours to hold it high.
   If ye break faith with us who die,
We shall not sleep, though poppies grow
      In Flanders fields.

ALUN LEWIS 1920-1944

ON A BEREAVED GIRL

She who yielded once
To the absolute of joy
Without the sanction of the Church
Is shrived now by the dying boy
Whose white absolving hands have laid
Silence upon her tongue and in her head.

She knows now in this grey
Negation of her life
That she can find no way
To lie beside him as his wife
And share his everlasting bed.

This further truth she knows—
Which Life must leave unsaid—
That the fled-away is eternal within her
And the devilry of the dead
Is also passionately flung away for ever
As she by hidden paths is led

By his deep silence summoned down
Through the sunken worlds of birth
Into the final grim delirium
Of the act of Death-on-Earth;
And deeper still, to where all action
Is sinless, sexless, and reverts
Into the slime of thought which rots away
The grafted skin and clinging cerements,
The little caves and meadows of the flesh,
And all the fond forgotten lineaments

And leaves the floating mesh,
The soul,
Some shape,
Unknown.

EDWARD L. DAVISON
NOCTURNE

Be thou at peace this night
   Wherever be thy bed,
Thy slumbering be light,
   The fearful dreams be dead
   Within thy lovely head;
God keep thee in His sight.

No hint of love molest
   Thy quiet mind again;
Night fold thee to her breast
   And hush thy crying pain;
   Let memory in vain
Conspire against thy rest.

So may thy thoughts be lost
   In the full hush of sleep.
Lest any sight accost
   Thine eyes to make them weep,
   In darkness buried deep
For ever be my ghost.

WILFRED OWEN 1893-1918
FUTILITY

Move him into the sun—
Gently its touch awoke him once,
At home, whispering of fields unsown.
Always it woke him, even in France,
Until this morning, and this snow.
If anything might rouse him now
The kind old sun will know.

Think how it wakes the seeds,—
Woke, once, the clays of a cold star.
Are limbs, so dear-achieved, are sides,
Full-nerved — still warm — too hard to stir?
Was it for this the clay grew tall?
— O what made fatuous sunbeams toil
To break earth's sleep at all?

IV

EDMUND BLUNDEN b. 1896

THE MEMORIAL
1914-1918

Against this lantern, shrill, alone
The wind springs out of the plain.
Such winds as this must fly and moan
Round the summit of every stone
On every hill; and yet a strain
Beyond the measure elsewhere known
Seems here.
        Who cries? Who mingles with the gale?
Whose touch, so anxious and so weak, invents
A coldness in the coldness? in this veil
Of whirling mist what hue of clay consents?
Can atoms intercede?

And are those shafted bold constructions there,
Mines more than golden, wheels that outrace need,
Crowded corons, victorious chimneys — are
Those touched with question too? pale with the dream
Of those who in this æther-stream
Are urging yet their painful, woundful theme?

Day flutters as a curtain, stirred
By a hidden hand; the eye grows blurred.
Those towns, uncrystalled, fade.
The wind from north and east and south
Comes with its starved white mouth
And at this crowning trophy cannot rest—
No, speaks as something past plain words distressed.

Be still, if these your voices are; this monolith
For you and your high sleep was made.
Some have had less.
No gratitude in deathlessness?
No comprehension of the tribute paid?

You would speak still? Who with?

DYLAN THOMAS b. 1914

THE HAND THAT SIGNED THE PAPER FELLED A CITY

The hand that signed the paper felled a city;
Five sovereign fingers taxed the breath,
Doubled the globe of dead and halved a country;
These five Kings did a King to death.

The mighty hand leads to a sloping shoulder,
The finger joints are cramped with chalk;
A goose's quill has put an end to murder
That put an end to talk.

The hand that signed the treaty bred a fever,
And famine grew, and locusts came;
Great is the hand that holds dominion over
Man by a scribbled name.

The five Kings count the dead but do not soften
The crusted wound nor pat the brow;
A hand rules pity as a hand rules heaven;
Hands have no tears to flow.

G. K. CHESTERTON 1874-1936
ELEGY IN A COUNTRY CHURCHYARD

The men that worked for England
They have their graves at home;
And bees and birds of England
About the cross can roam.

But they that fought for England,
Following a falling star,
Alas, alas for England
They have their graves afar.

And they that rule in England,
In stately conclave met,
Alas, alas for England
They have no graves as yet.

RUDYARD KIPLING 1865-1936
MESOPOTAMIA 1917

They shall not return to us, the resolute, the young,
    The eager and whole-hearted whom we gave:
But the men who left them thriftily to die in their own dung,
    Shall they come with years and honour to the grave?

They shall not return to us, the strong men coldly slain
    In sight of help denied from day to day:
But the men who edged their agonies and chid them in their pain,
    Are they too strong and wise to put away?

Our dead shall not return to us while Day and Night divide—
    Never while the bars of sunset hold.
But the idle-minded overlings who quibbled while they died,
    Shall they thrust for high employments as of old?

Shall we only threaten and be angry for an hour?
   When the storm is ended shall we find
How softly but how swiftly they have sidled back to power
   By the favour and contrivance of their kind?

Even while they soothe us, while they promise large amends,
   Even while they make a show of fear,
Do they call upon their debtors, and take counsel with their friends,
   To confirm and re-establish each career?

Their lives cannot repay us — their death could not undo —
   The shame that they have laid upon our race.
But the slothfulness that wasted and the arrogance that slew,
   Shall we leave it unabated in its place?

WILLIAM WORDSWORTH 1770-1850

NOVEMBER
1806

Another year! — another deadly blow!
Another mighty Empire overthrown!
And We are left, or shall be left, alone;
The last that dare to struggle with the Foe.
'Tis well! from this day forward we shall know
That in ourselves our safety must be sought;
That by our own right hands it must be wrought;
That we must stand unpropped, or be laid low.
O dastard whom such foretaste doth not cheer!
We shall exult, if they who rule the land
Be men who hold its many blessings dear,
Wise, upright, valiant; not the servile band,
Who are to judge of danger which they fear,
And honour which they do not understand.

LORD BYRON 1788-1824
STANZAS

When a man hath no freedom to fight for at home,
    Let him combat for that of his neighbours;
Let him think of the glories of Greece and of Rome,
    And get knocked on the head for his labours.

To do good to mankind is the chivalrous plan,
    And is always as nobly requited;
Then battle for freedom wherever you can,
    And, if not shot or hanged, you'll get knighted.

EDWARD THOMAS 1878-1917
THIS IS NO CASE OF PETTY RIGHT OR WRONG

This is no case of petty right or wrong
That politicians or philosophers
Can judge. I hate not Germans, nor grow hot
With love of Englishmen, to please newspapers.
Beside my hate for one fat patriot
My hatred of the Kaiser is love true:—
A kind of god he is, banging a gong.
But I have not to choose between the two,
Or between justice and injustice. Dinned
With war and argument I read no more
Than in the storm smoking along the wind
Athwart the wood. Two witches' cauldrons roar.
From one the weather shall rise clear and gay;
Out of the other an England beautiful
And like her mother that died yesterday.
Little I know or care if, being dull,
I shall miss something that historians
Can rake out of the ashes when perchance

The phœnix broods serene above their ken.
But with the best and meanest Englishmen
I am one in crying, God save England, lest
We lose what never slaves and cattle blessed.
The ages made her that made us from dust:
She is all we know and live by, and we trust
She is good and must endure, loving her so:
And as we love ourselves we hate her foe.

ALAN ROOK b. 1913

DUNKIRK PIER

Deeply across the waves of our darkness fear,
like the silent octopus, feeling, groping, clear
as a star's reflection, nervous and cold as a bird,
tells us that pain, tells us that death is near.

Why should a woman telling above her fire
incantations of evening, thoughts that are
older and paler than history, why should this lark
exploring extinction and oneness of self and air

remind us that, lonely and lost as flowers in deserted
weed-mastered gardens, each faint face averted
from the inescapable confusion, for each of us slowly
death on his last, most hideous journey has started?

What was our sin? — that heartless to the end
falls now the heavy sickle on foe, on friend,
and those that we love, value and regret
surrender quickest to death's empty hand.

Failure to suffer? We who in years past
have suffered, yes, in this or that, but in the last
irrevocable act of suffering, as a dog suffers deeply,
blindly, completely, are not versed.

What hope for the future ? Can we who see the tide
ebbing along the shore, the greedy, lined
with shadows, dare with puny words support
a future which belongs to others ? Dare we bind

now, at this last moment of sunshine above
the crests of oncoming events, like waves which move
remorselessly nearer, future generations
with sacrifice? *We* who taught hate, expect them to love?

SAMUEL TAYLOR COLERIDGE 1772 - 1834

FEARS IN SOLITUDE

A green and silent spot, amid the hills,
A small and silent dell! O'er stiller place
No singing skylark ever poised himself.
The hills are heathy, save that swelling slope,
Which hath a gay and gorgeous covering on
All golden with the never-bloomless furze,
Which now blooms most profusely: but the dell,
Bathed by the mist, is fresh and delicate
As vernal cornfield, or the unripe flax,
When, through its half-transparent stalks, at eve,
The level sunshine glimmers with green light.
Oh! 'tis a quiet spirit-healing nook!
Which all, methinks, would love; but chiefly he,
The humble man, who, in his youthful years,
Knew just so much of folly, as has made
His early manhood more securely wise!
Here he might lie on fern or withered heath,
While from the singing lark (that sings unseen
The minstrelsy that solitude loves best),
And from the sun, and from the breezy air,
Sweet influences trembled o'er his frame;

And he, with many feelings, many thoughts,
Made up a meditative joy, and found
Religious meanings in the forms of Nature!
And so, his senses gradually wrapt
In a half sleep, he dreams of better worlds,
And dreaming hears thee still, o singing lark;
That singest like an angel in the clouds!

My God! it is a melancholy thing
For such a man, who would full fain preserve
His soul in calmness, yet perforce must feel
For all his human brethren — O my God!
It weighs upon the heart, that he must think
What uproar and what strife may now be stirring
This way or that way o'er these silent hills—
Invasion, and the thunder and the shout,
And all the crash of onset; fear and rage,
And undetermined conflict — even now,
Even now, perchance, and in his native isle:
Carnage and groans beneath this blessed sun!
We have offended, Oh! my countrymen!
We have offended very grievously,
And been most tyrannous. From east to west
A groan of accusation pierces Heaven!
The wretched plead against us; multitudes
Countless and vehement, the sons of God,
Our brethren! Like a cloud that travels on,
Steamed up from Cairo's swamps of pestilence,
Even so, my countrymen! have we gone forth
And borne to distant tribes slavery and pangs,
And, deadlier far, our vices, whose deep taint
With slow perdition murders the whole man,
His body and his soul! Meanwhile, at home,
All individual dignity and power
Engulfed in Courts, Committees, Institutions,
Associations and Societies,
A vain, speech-mouthing, speech-reporting Guild,
One Benefit-Club for mutual flattery,

We have drunk up, demure as at a grace,
Pollutions from the brimming cup of wealth;
Contemptuous of all honourable rule,
Yet bartering freedom and the poor man's life
For gold, as at a market! The sweet words
Of Christian promise, words that even yet
Might stem destruction, were they wisely preached,
Are mutter'd o'er by men, whose tones proclaim
How flat and wearisome they feel their trade:
Rank scoffers some, but most too indolent
To deem them falsehoods or to know their truth.
Oh! blasphemous! the Book of Life is made
A superstitious instrument, on which
We gabble o'er the oaths we mean to break;
For all must swear — all and in every place,
College and wharf, council and justice-court;
All, all must swear, the briber and the bribed,
Merchant and lawyer, senator and priest,
The rich, the poor, the old man and the young;
All, all make up one scheme of perjury,
That faith doth reel; the very name of God
Sounds like a juggler's charm; and, bold with joy,
Forth from his dark and lonely hiding-place,
(Portentous sight!) the owlet Atheism,
Sailing on obscene wings athwart the noon,
Drops his blue-fringed lids, and holds them close,
And hooting at the glorious sun in Heaven,
Cries out, "Where is it?"

      Thankless too for peace,
(Peace long preserved by fleets and perilous seas)
Secure from actual warfare, we have loved
To swell the war-whoop, passionate for war!
Alas! for ages ignorant of all
Its ghastlier workings (famine or blue plague,
Battle, or siege, or flight through wintry snows)
We, this whole people, have been clamorous
For war and bloodshed; animating sports,

The which we pay for as a thing to talk of,
Spectators and not combatants! No guess
Anticipative of a wrong unfelt,
No speculation on contingency,
However dim and vague, too vague and dim
To yield a justifying cause; and forth,
(Stuffed out with big preamble, holy names,
And adjurations of the God of Heaven)
We send our mandates for the certain death
Of thousands and ten thousands! Boys and girls,
And women that would groan to see a child
Pull off an insect's leg, all read of war
The best amusement for our morning meal!
The poor wretch, who has learnt his only prayers
From curses, who knows scarcely words enough
To ask a blessing from his Heavenly Father,
Becomes a fluent phraseman, absolute
And technical in victories and defeats,
And all our dainty terms for fratricide;
Terms which we trundle smoothly o'er our tongues
Like mere abstractions, empty sounds to which
We join no feeling and attach no form!
As if the soldier died without a wound;
As if the fibres of this godlike frame
Were gored without a pang; as if the wretch,
Who fell in battle, doing bloody deeds,
Passed off to Heaven, translated and not killed!
As though he had no wife to pine for him,
No God to judge him! Therefore, evil days
Are coming on us, O my countrymen!
And what if all-avenging Providence
Strong and retributive, should make us know
The meaning of our words, force us to feel
The desolation and the agony
Of our fierce doings?
      Spare us yet a while,
Father and God! O! Spare us yet awhile,
Oh! let not English women drag their flight

Fainting beneath the burthen of their babes,
Of the sweet infants that but yesterday
Laughed at the breast! Sons, brothers, husbands, all
Who ever gazed with fondness on the forms
Which grew up with you round the same fireside,
And all who ever heard the sabbath-bells
Without the infidel's scorn, make yourselves pure!
Stand forth! be men! repel an impious foe,
Impious and false, a light yet cruel race,
Who laugh away all virtue, mingling mirth
With deeds of murder; and still promising
Freedom, themselves too sensual to be free,
Poison life's amities, and cheat the heart
Of faith and quiet hope, and all that soothes
And all that lifts the spirit! Stand we forth;
Render them back upon the insulted ocean,
And let them toss as idly on its waves
As the vile sea-weed, which some mountain-blast
Swept from our shores! And oh! may we return
Not with a drunken triumph, but with fear,
Repenting of the wrongs with which we stung
So fierce a foe to frenzy!

     I have told,
O Britons! O my brethren! I have told
Most bitter truth, but without bitterness.
Nor deem my zeal or factious or mistimed;
For never can true courage dwell with them,
Who, playing tricks with conscience, dare not look
At their own vices. We have been too long
Dupes of a deep delusion! Some, belike,
Groaning with restless enmity, expect
All change from change of constituted power;
As if a Government had been a robe,
On which our vice and wretchedness were tagged
Like fancy-points and fringes, with the robe
Pulled off at pleasure. Fondly these attach
A radical causation to a few

Poor drudges of chastising Providence,
Who borrow all their hues and qualities
From our own folly and rank wickedness,
Which gave them birth and nursed them. Others, meanwhile,
Dote with a mad idolatry; and all
Who will not fall before their images,
And yield them worship, they are enemies
Even of their country!

                Such have I been deemed.—
But, O, dear Britain! O my Mother Isle!
Needs must thou prove a name most dear and holy
To me, a son, a brother, and a friend.
A husband and a father! who revere
All bonds of natural love, and find them all
Within the limits of thy rocky shores.
O native Britain! O my Mother Isle!
How shouldst thou prove aught else but dear and holy
To me, who from thy lakes and mountain-hills,
Thy clouds, thy quiet dales, thy rocks and seas,
Have drunk in all my intellectual life,
All sweet sensations, all ennobling thoughts,
All adoration of the God in nature,
All lovely and all honourable things,
Whatever makes this mortal spirit feel
The joy and greatness of its future being?
There lives nor form nor feeling in my soul
Unborrowed from my country. O divine
And beauteous island! thou hast been my sole
And most magnificent temple, in the which
I walk with awe, and sing my stately songs,
Loving the God that made me!—
                            May my fears,
My filial fears, be vain! and may the vaunts
And menace of the vengeful enemy
Pass like the gust, that roared and died away
In the distant tree: which heard, and only heard
In this low dell, bowed not the delicate grass.

But now the gentle dew-fall sends abroad
The fruit-like perfume of the golden furze;
The light has left the summit of the hill,
Though still a sunny gleam lies beautiful,
Aslant the ivied beacon. Now farewell,
Farewell, awhile, O soft and silent spot!
On the green sheep-track, up the heathy hill,
Homeward I wind my way; and lo! recalled
From bodings that have well-nigh wearied me,
I find myself upon the brow, and pause
Startled! And after lonely sojourning
In such a quiet and surrounded nook,
This burst of prospect here, the shadowy main,
Dim-tinted, there the mighty majesty
Of that huge amphitheatre of rich
And elmy fields, seems like society—
Conversing with the mind and giving it
A livelier impulse and a dance of thought!
And now, beloved Stowey! I behold
Thy church-tower, and, methinks, the four huge elms
Clustering, which mark the mansion of my friend;
And close behind them, hidden from my view,
Is my own lowly cottage, where my babe
And my babe's mother dwell in peace! With light
And quickening footsteps thitherward I tend,
Remembering thee, O green and silent dell!
And grateful, that by nature's quietness
And solitary musings, all my heart
Is softened, and made worthy to indulge
Love, and the thoughts that yearn for human kind.

VII

WALTER SAVAGE LANDOR 1775-1864
A FOREIGN RULER

He says, *my reign is peace,* so slays
   A thousand in the dead of night.
Are you all happy now? he says
   And those he leaves behind cry *quite.*
He swears he will have no contention,
   And sets all nature by the ears;
He shouts aloud, *No intervention!*
   Invades, and drowns them all in tears.

WALTER DE LA MARE b. 1873
NAPOLEON

'What is the world, O soldiers?
    It is I:
I, this incessant snow,
    This northern sky;
Soldiers, this solitude
    Through which we go
      Is I.'

ROBERT BROWNING 1812-1889
INCIDENT OF THE FRENCH CAMP

You know, we French stormed Ratisbon:
    A mile or so away,
On a little mound, Napoleon
    Stood on our storming day;
With neck out-thrust, you fancy how,
    Legs wide, arms locked behind,
As if to balance the prone brow
    Oppressive with its mind.

Just as perhaps he mused 'My plans
    'That soar, to earth may fall,
'Let once my army-leader, Lannes
    'Waver at yonder wall,'—
Out twixt the battery-smokes there flew
    A rider, bound on bound
Full-galloping; nor bridle drew
    Until he reached the mound.

Then off there flung in smiling joy,
    And held himself erect
By just his horse's mane, a boy:
    You hardly could suspect—
(So tight he kept his lips compressed,
    Scarce any blood came through)
You looked twice ere you saw his breast
    Was all but shot in two.

'Well,' cried he, 'Emperor, by God's grace
    'We've got you Ratisbon!
'The Marshal's in the market-place,
    'And you'll be there anon
'To see your flag-bird flap his vans
    'Where I, to heart's desire,
'Perched him!' The chief's eye flashed; his plans
    Soared up again like fire.

  The chief's eye flashed: but presently
   Softened itself, as sheathes
  A film the mother-eagle's eye
   When her bruised eaglet breathes;
  'You're wounded!' 'Nay,' the soldier's pride
   Touched to the quick, he said:
  'I'm killed, Sire!' And his chief beside
   Smiling the boy fell dead.

R. L. STEVENSON 1850-1894

A MARTIAL ELEGY FOR SOME LEAD SOLDIERS

  For certain soldiers lately dead
  Our reverent dirge shall here be said.
  Them, when their martial leader called,
  No dread preparative appalled;
  But leaden-hearted, leaden-heeled,
  I marked them steadfast in the field.
  Death grimly sided with the foe,
  And smote each leaden hero low.
  Proudly they perished one by one:
  The dread Pea-cannon's work was done!
  O not for them the tears we shed,
  Consigned to their congenial lead;
  But while unmoved their sleep they take,
  We mourn for their dear Captain's sake,
  For their dear Captain, who shall smart
  Both in his pocket and in his heart,
  Who saw his heroes shed their gore
  And lacked a shilling to buy more!

WILLIAM WORDSWORTH 1770-1850
SONNET

The Column Intended by Buonaparte for a Triumphal Edifice in Milan, now Lying by the Way-side in the Simplon Pass

Ambition — following down this far-famed slope
Her Pioneer, the snow-dissolving Sun,
While clarions prate of kingdoms to be won—
Perchance, in future ages, here may stop;
Taught to mistrust her flattering horoscope
By admonition from this prostrate Stone!
Memento uninscribed of Pride o'erthrown,
Vanity's hieroglyphic; a choice trope
In Fortune's rhetoric. Daughter of the Rock,
Rest where thy course was stayed by Power divine!
The Soul transported sees, from hint of thine,
Crimes which the great Avenger's hand provoke,
Hears combats whistling o'er the ensanguined heath:
What groans! what shrieks! what quietness in death!

W. E. AYTOUN 1813-1865
SONNET TO BRITAIN

Halt! Shoulder arms! Recover! As you were!
  Right wheel! Eyes left! Attention! Stand at ease!
  O Britain! O my country! Words like these
Have made thy name a terror and a fear
To all the nations. Witness Ebro's banks,
  Assaye, Toulouse, Nivelle, and Waterloo,
  Where the grim despot muttered — *Sauve qui peut*!
And Ney fled darkling. — Silence in the ranks!

Inspired by these, amidst the iron crash
  Of armies, in the centre of his troop
The soldier stands — unmovable, not rash—
  Until the forces of the foeman droop;
Then knocks the Frenchmen to eternal smash,
  Pounding them into mummy. Shoulder, Hoop!

WINTHROP MACKWORTH PRAED 1802-1839
WATERLOO

Ay, here such valorous deeds were done
 As ne'er were done before;
Ay, here the reddest wreath was won
 That ever Gallia wore;
Since Ariosto's wondrous Knight
 Made all the Paynims dance,
There never dawned a day so bright
 As Waterloo's on France.

The trumpet poured its deafening sound,
 Flags fluttered on the gale,
And cannon roared, and heads flew round
 As fast as summer hail;
The sabres flashed their light of fear,
 The steeds began to prance;
The English quaked from front to rear—
 They never quake in France!

The cuirassiers rode in and out
 As fierce as wolves and bears;
'Twas grand to see them slash about
 Among the English squares!
And then the Polish Lancer came
 Careering with his lance;
No wonder Britain blushed for shame,
 And ran away from France!

The Duke of York was killed that day;
 The king was sadly scarred;
Lord Eldon, as he ran away,
 Was taken by the Guard;
Poor Wellington with fifty Blues
 Escaped by some strange chance;
Henceforth I think he'll hardly choose
 To show himself in France.

So Buonaparte pitched his tent
   That night in Grosvenor Place,
And Ney rode straight to Parliament
   And broke the Speaker's mace;
"Vive l'Empereur" was said and sung
   From Peebles to Penzance;
The Mayor and Aldermen were hung;
   Which made folk laugh in France.

They pulled the Tower of London down,
   They burnt our wooden walls;
They brought the Pope himself to town,
   And lodged him in St. Paul's;
And Gog and Magog rubbed their eyes,
   Awaking from a trance,
And grumbled out, in great surprise,
   "Oh, mercy! we're in France!"

They sent a Regent to our Isle,
   The little King of Rome;
And squibs and crackers all the while
   Blazed in the Place Vendôme;
And ever since, in arts and power,
   They're making great advance;
They've had strong beer from that glad hour,
   And sea-coal fires, in France.

My uncle, Captain Flanigan,
   Who lost a leg in Spain,
Tells stories of a little man
   Who died at St. Helene;
But bless my heart, they can't be true;
   I'm sure they're all romance;
John Bull was beat at Waterloo!
   They'll swear to that in France.

T. S. ELIOT b. 1888

TRIUMPHAL MARCH

Stone, bronze, stone, steel, stone, oakleaves, horses' heels
Over the paving.
And the flags. And the trumpets. And so many eagles.
How many? Count them. And such a press of people.
We hardly knew ourselves that day or knew the City.
This is the way to the temple, and we so many crowding the way.
So many waiting, how many waiting? What did it matter, on
such a day?

Are they coming? No, not yet. You can see some eagles.
And hear the trumpets.
Here they come. Is he coming?
The natural wakeful life of our Ego is a perceiving.
We can wait with our stools and our sausages.
What comes first? Can you see? Tell us. It is

     5,800,000 rifles and carbines,
     102,000 machine guns,
     28,000 trench mortars,
     53,000 field and heavy guns,
I cannot tell how many projectiles, mines, and fuses,
     13,000 aeroplanes,
     24,000 aeroplane engines,
     50,000 ammunition waggons,
  now 55,000 army waggons,
     11,000 field kitchens,
     1,150 field bakeries.

What a time that took. Will it be he now? No,
Those are the golf club Captains, these the Scouts,
And now the *Société gymnastique de Poissy*
And now come the Mayor and the Liverymen. Look
There is he now, look:
There is no interrogation in his eyes
Or in the hands, quiet over the horse's neck,

And the eyes watchful, waiting, perceiving, indifferent.
O hidden under the dove's wing, hidden in the turtle's breast,
Under the palmtree at noon, under the running water
At the still point of the turning world.   O hidden.

Now they go up to the Temple.   Then the sacrifice.
Now come the virgins bearing urns, urns containing
Dust
Dust
Dust of dust, and now
Stone, bronze, stone, steel, stone, oakleaves, horses' heels
Over the paving.

That is all we could see. But how many eagles and how many
    trumpets!
(And Easter Day, we didn't get to the country,
So we took young Cyril to church.   And they rang a bell
And he said right out loud, *crumpets*.)

It'll come in handy.   He's artful.   Please, will you
Give us a light?
Light
Light
Et les soldats faisaient la haie?   ILS LA FAISAIENT.

SIR EDWARD MARSH
CŒLO TONANTEM
TRANSLATED FROM THE LATIN OF HORACE: ODES III. 5

Jove thundered out of heaven, and straight was known
   Earth's monarch: so shall Cæsar stand revealed
Apparent God, when, East and West o'erthrown,
   Britain and Persia to his rule shall yield.

How then could Crassus' vanquished soldiery,
   Sons of the Senate, bred to Roman ways,
Wive with their captors' women, live and die
   Drilled by old foes, new kinsmen, all their days,

Marsians, Apulians, thrall to Medish kings,
   Forgetful of the name, the robe, the blood,
And Numa's shield, and Vesta's holy things,
   And living Rome where yet Jove's altar stood?

Such foul dishonour Regulus foresaw
   Unending, were the foeman's proffered grace
Not spurned; such presage could his wisdom draw
   Of long disaster to a falling race,

If pity for the captive youth prevailed;
   And thus his words found way: 'These eyes have known
Our standards in the shrines of Carthage trailed,
   Our men, unwounded, lay their weapons down,

Free men of Rome, arms pinioned to their side,
   To slavery marched where once they marched to war;
Gates that have braved our leaguer, standing wide,
   And fields our fire had wasted, sown once more.

Bought back with gold, they will return, you say,
   With doubled spirit? Oh folly heaped on blame!
Your wool discoloured, dye it as you may,
   Will it regain its hue, and be the same?

No, nor true valour, once driven out and spoiled,
  Deigns in her ruined seat to dwell again.
Show me the stag, once in the nets entoiled,
  Will fight another bout, and tell me then

That he who parleyed with a treacherous foe,
  And felt the thong upon his limbs, and lay
Passive in craven fear of death, will go
  Forth to destroy him in a second fray.

Oh base, to seek for life where no life is,
  And peace with war confound! Oh depth of shame!
Oh mighty Carthage, first of enemies,
  Who on Rome's downfall buildest up thy fame!'

'Tis told, that when his wife and little sons
  Came with their kisses, he, as one disowned,
Put them away, nor looked upon them once,
  But sternly fixed his eyes upon the ground,

Strengthened the hesitant Fathers to obey
  His word, self-doomed as never man but he;
Then through his weeping kin he took his way
  To exile, and to immortality.

Full well he knew what pains he must abide,
  The torturer's devilry, the screw, the wrack,
Yet gently thrust his clamouring friends aside,
  And the fond crowd that strove to hold him back,

Just as of old, the long day's business done,
  His clients served, he started on his way
To green Venafrum by the setting sun,
  Or the calms folds of the Calabrian bay.

ALFRED LORD TENNYSON 1809-1892

TO GENERAL HAMLEY

Our birches yellowing and from each
    The light leaf falling fast,
While squirrels from our fiery beech
    Were bearing off the mast,
You came, and looked and loved the view
    Long-known and loved by me,
Green Sussex fading into blue
    With one gray glimpse of sea;
And, gazing from this height alone,
    We spoke of what had been
Most marvellous in the wars your own
    Crimean eyes had seen;
And now—like old-world inns that take
    Some warrior for a sign
That therewithin a guest may make
    True cheer with honest wine—
Because you heard the lines I read
    Nor uttered word of blame,
I dare without your leave to head
    These rhymings with your name,
Who know you but as one of those
    I fain would meet again,
Yet know you, as your England knows
    That you and all your men
Were soldiers to her heart's desire
    When, in the vanished year,
You saw the league-long rampart-fire
    Flare from Tel-el-Kebir
Thro' darkness, and the foe was driven,
    And Wolseley overthrew
Arâbi and the stars in heaven
    Paled, and the glory grew.

WALTER DE LA MARE b. 1873
THE OLD SOLDIER

There came an Old Soldier to my door,
Asked a crust, and asked no more;
The wars had thinned him very bare,
Fighting and marching everywhere,
    With a Fol rol dol rol di do.

With nose stuck out, and cheek sunk in,
A bristling beard upon his chin—
Powder and bullets and wounds and drums
Had come to that Soldier as suchlike comes—
    With a Fol rol dol rol di do.

'Twas sweet and fresh with buds of May,
Flowers springing from every spray;
And when he had supped the Old Soldier trolled
The song of youth that never grows old,
    Called Fol rol dol rol di do.

Most of him rags, and all of him lean,
And the belt round his belly drawn tightsome in,
He lifted his peaked old grizzled head,
And these were the very same words he said—
    A Fol-rol-dol-rol-*di*-do.

ANONYMOUS C.1660

AN OLD SOULDIER OF THE QUEENS
from
MERRY DROLLERY

Of an old Souldier of the Queens,
With an old motley coat, and a Maumsie nose,
And an old Jerkin that's out at the elbows,
And an old pair of boots, drawn on without hose
Stuft with rags instead of toes;
    And an old Souldier of the Queens,
    And the Queens old Souldier.

With an old rusty sword that's hackt with blows,
And an old dagger to scare away the crows,
And an old horse that reels as he goes,
And an old saddle that no man knows,
    And an old Souldier of the Queens,
    And the Queens old Souldier.

With his old wounds in Eighty Eight,
Which he recover'd, at *Tilbury* fight;
With an old Pasport that never was read,
That in his old travels stood him in great stead;
    And an old Souldier of the Queens,
    And the Queens old Souldier.

With his old Gun, and his Bandeliers,
And an old head-piece to keep warm his ears,
With an old shirt is grown to wrack,
With a huge Louse, with a great list on his back,
Is able to carry a Pedlar and his Pack;
    And an old Souldier of the Queens,
    And the Queens old Souldier.

With an old Quean to lie by his side,
That in old time had been pockifi'd;
He's now rid to *Bohemia* to fight with his foes,
And he swears by his Valour he'll have better cloaths,
Or else he'll lose legs, arms, fingers, and toes,
And he'll come again, when no man knows,
    And an old Souldier of the Queens,
    And the Queens old Souldier.

w. s. gilbert 1836-1911

THE MODERN MAJOR-GENERAL

I am the very pattern of a modern Major-General,
I've information vegetable, animal, and mineral;
I know the kings of England, and I quote the fights historical,
From Marathon to Waterloo, in order categorical;
I'm very well acquainted, too, with matters mathematical,
I understand equations, both the simple and quadratical;
About binomial theorem I'm teeming with a lot o' news,
With interesting facts about the square of the hypotenuse.
I'm very good at integral and differential calculus,
I know the scientific names of beings animalculous.
In short, in matters vegetable, animal, and mineral,
I am the very model of a modern Major-Gineral.

I know our mythic history—KING ARTHUR'S and SIR CARADOC'S,
I answer hard acrostics, I've a pretty taste for paradox;
I quote in elegiacs all the crimes of HELIOGABALUS,
In conics I can floor peculiarities parabolous.
I tell undoubted RAPHAELS from GERARD DOWS and ZOFFANIES,
I know the croaking chorus from the "Frogs" of ARISTOPHANES;
Then I can hum a fugue, of which I've heard the music's din afore,
And whistle all the airs from that confounded nonsense "Pinafore."

Then I can write a washing-bill in Babylonic cuneiform,
And tell you every detail of CARACTACUS's uniform.
In short, in matters vegetable, animal, and mineral,
I am the very model of a modern Major-Gineral.

In fact, when I know what is meant by "mamelon" and "ravelin,"
When I can tell at sight a Chassepôt rifle from a javelin,
When such affairs as *sorties* and surprises I'm more wary at,
And when I know precisely what is meant by Commissariat,
When I have learnt what progress has been made in modern gunnery,
When I know more of tactics than a novice in a nunnery,
In short, when I've a smattering of elementary strategy,
You'll say a better Major-Gine*ral* has never *sat* a gee—
For my military knowledge, though I'm plucky and adventury,
Has only been brought down to the beginning of the century.
But still in learning vegetable, animal, and mineral,
I am the very model of a modern Major-Gineral!

VIII

W. B. YEATS 1865-1939

THE ROAD AT MY DOOR

An affable Irregular
A heavily-built Falstaffian man,
Comes cracking jokes of civil war
As though to die by gunshot were
The finest play under the sun.

A brown Lieutenant and his men,
Half dressed in national uniform,
Stand at my door, and I complain
Of the foul weather, hail and rain,
A peartree broken by the storm.

I count those feathered balls of soot
The moor-hen guides upon the stream
To silence the envy in my thought;
And turn towards my chamber, caught
In the cold snows of a dream.

G. ROSTREVOR HAMILTON b. 1888

APOLLYON

How shall unsainted John
Fight that Apollyon,
William the plain man
And Frank the sane man
His fire-darts parry?
How shall we decent men,
Tom, Dick and Harry,
Firm though our will,
Fortitude, skill,
Hope to cope with and overthrow
A maniac foe,
Ravings and cold-blood deeds that glow
With fires of evil beyond our ken,
Deliberate murderers, furious liars?

Matched with extremest lies,
Weak is our compromise;
Wholeness of dark sin,
Or pride of stark sin
From hope of God parted,
Jeer at our virtue's mean,
Mock the good-hearted;
Hate and despair
Ride on the air,
Camp, and trample the earth and seize
What forfeit they please,
Freedom, honour, from dwellers at ease;
While, yeomen at bay, we fend us between
A God half-forgotten and Hell-driven foemen.

Fight we no mortal foes
Only; from Hell there goes,
Prince of all evil,
The banqueted Devil:

Grand cosmopolitan,
Diplomat everywhere,
Sleek man or jolly man;
Wearing disguise,
Circumspect, wise,
Dulling and lulling us, teaching the soul
His moderate rôle,
Respectability's aureole;
Abolishing sin with a smooth veneer
And social disease with a brand-new polish.

One and the same is he
Through all variety,
Whether he drowse us
With syrup, or rouse us
With venom of fury;
Proffer to each plain
Member of jury,
Pillar of State,
Churchman sedate,
Piety's diet of flat routine,
Or terrible wine
Pour for his chosen, for those who dine
At the gory banquet of Liberty slain,
Lusty lieutenants who share his glory.

Foulness and filth are done
Under the mid-day sun;
Itching dreamers
And loud blasphemers
Hail 'love' where lust is,
Christen a nameless
Cruelty 'justice'.
Nations who bleed
Cry to be freed.
How shall we now, at the last, last hour
Withstand this power,
We, with moderate virtue for dower?

And reason and manners and mild address,
How shall they parley with insolent treason?

Though we defeat at length
Men and their fleshly strength,
Still the evangel
Of Hell's dark angel
Trumpets him master.
Rises the Arch-fiend
Big with disaster;
Sleep and sin
Betray us within—
O God, let thy rod chastise and break us,
Wild men wake us,
Saints in extremity mar and make us!
Teach us extremes, who once didst send
Thy well-loved Son, through death to reach us,

Teach us, as He in death did feel
The antagonist's bruise upon His heel,
Yet dying bruised that horned head
And rose a conqueror from the dead,
Teach us, who feel Earth's anguished wrong,
A good that's more extreme and strong
Than evil; rouse in us that good
Through His Cross and through His Blood.

EDMUND BLUNDEN b. 1896

SOME TALK OF PEACE —

Dark War, exploding loud mephitic mines
Or with a single shot destroying twenty,
Was in a way reserved, polite and dainty.
Then there was not much felt of cold designs,
Murder that chanced seemed past man's guiding-lines,
And conscience never flushed for that grim throe.

Peace, lovely lady, is too fine to shout
Her power abroad; she seldom lays us low
As the machine-guns stretched the storm-troops out;
She gives us time to answer Yes or No.
She may not kill; she even keeps alive
Those whom their faces or their foes deprive
Of joy and equity; and we live in doubt
Whether her sins or War's more misery sow.

W. J. TURNER b. 1889

TALKING WITH SOLDIERS

The mind of the people is like mud,
From which arise strange and beautiful things,
But mud is none the less mud,
Though it bear orchids and prophesying Kings,
Dreams, trees, and water's bright babblings.

It has found form and colour and light,
The cold glimmer of the ice-wrapped Poles;
It has called a far-off glow Arcturus,
And some pale weeds, lilies of the valley.

It has imagined Virgil, Helen and Cassandra;
The sack of Troy, and the weeping for Hector—

Rearing stark up 'mid all this beauty
In the thick, dull neck of Ajax.

There is a dark Pine in Lapland,
And the great, figured Horn of the Reindeer
Moving soundlessly across the snow,
Is its twin brother, double-dreamed,
In the mind of a far-off people.

It is strange that a little mud
Should echo with sounds, syllables, and letters,
Should rise up and call a mountain Popocatapetl,
And a green leafed wood Oleander.

These are the ghosts of invisible things;
There is no Lapland, no Helen and no Hector,
And the Reindeer is a darkening of the brain,
And Oleander is but Oleander.

Mary Magdalena and the vine Lachrymae Christi,
Were like ghosts up the ghost of Vesuvius,
As I sat and drank wine with the soldiers,
As I sat in the Inn on the mountain,
Watching the shadows in my mind.

The mind of the people is like mud:
Where are the imperishable things,
The ghosts that flicker in the brain—
Silent women, orchids, and prophesying Kings,
Dreams, trees, and water's bright babblings?

W. H. AUDEN b. 1907
REFUGEE BLUES

Say this city has ten million souls,
Some are living in mansions, some are living in holes:
Yet there's no place for us, my dear, yet there's no place for us.

Once we had a country and we thought it fair,
Look in the atlas and you'll find it there:
We cannot go there now, my dear, we cannot go there now.

In the village churchyard there grows an old yew,
Every spring it blossoms anew:
Old passports can't do that, my dear, old passports can't do that.

The consul banged the table and said;
'If you've got no passport you're officially dead':
But we are still alive, my dear, but we are still alive.

Went to a committee; they offered me a chair;
Asked me politely to return next year:
But where shall we go today, my dear, but where shall we go today?

Came to a public meeting; the speaker got up and said:
'If we let them in, they will steal our daily bread';
He was talking of you and me, my dear, he was talking of you and me.

Thought I heard the thunder rumbling in the sky,
It was Hitler over Europe, saying: 'They must die';
O we were in his mind, my dear, O we were in his mind.

Saw a poodle in a jacket fastened with a pin,
Saw a door opened and a cat let in:
But they weren't German Jews, my dear, but they weren't German Jews.

Went down the harbour and stood upon the quay,
Saw the fish swimming as if they were free:
Only ten feet away, my dear, only ten feet away.

Walked through a wood, saw the birds in the trees;
They had no politicians and sang at their ease:
They weren't the human race, my dear, they weren't the human race.

Dreamed I saw a building with a thousand floors,
A thousand windows and a thousand doors;
Not one of them was ours, my dear, not one of them was ours.

Stood on a great plain in the falling snow;
Ten thousand soldiers marched to and fro:
Looking for you and me, my dear, looking for you and me.

ANONYMOUS. WRITTEN 809 A.D.
Translated from the Chinese by Arthur Waley

THE PRISONER

Tartars led in chains,
Tartars led in chains!
Their ears pierced, their faces bruised—they are driven into the land of Ch'in.
The Son of Heaven took pity on them and would not have them slain.
He sent them away to the south-east, to the lands of Wu and Yüeh.
A petty officer in a yellow coat took down their names and surnames:
They were led from the city of Ch'ang-an under escort of an armed guard.
Their bodies were covered with the wounds of arrows, their bones stood out from their cheeks.
They had grown so weak they could only march a single stage a day.
In the morning they must satisfy hunger and thirst with neither plate nor cup:
At night they must lie in their dirt and rags on beds that stank with filth.

Suddenly they came to the Yangtze River and remembered the
   waters of Chiao.
With lowered hands and levelled voices they sobbed a muffled song.
Then one Tartar lifted up his voice and spoke to the other Tartars,
"*Your* sorrows are none at all compared with *my* sorrows."
Those that were with him in the same band asked to hear his tale:
As he tried to speak the words were choked by anger.
He told them "I was born and bred in the town of Liang-yüan.
In the frontier wars of Ta-li I fell into the Tartars' hands.
Since the days the Tartars took me alive forty years have passed:
They put me into a coat of skins tied with a belt of rope.
Only on the first of the first month might I wear my Chinese dress.
As I put on my coat and arranged my cap, how fast the tears flowed!
I made in my heart a secret vow I would find a way home:
I hid my plan from my Tartar wife and the children she had borne
   me in the land.
I thought to myself, 'It is well for me that my limbs are still strong,'
And yet, being old, in my heart I feared I should never live to return.
The Tartar chieftains shoot so well that the birds are afraid to fly:
From the risk of their arrows I escaped alive and fled swiftly home.
Hiding all day and walking all night, I crossed the Great Desert:
Where clouds are dark and the moon black and the sands eddy in
   the wind.
Frightened, I sheltered at the Green Grave, where the frozen grasses
   are few:
Stealthily I crossed the Yellow River, at night, on the thin ice,
Suddenly I heard Han drums and the sound of soldiers coming:
I went to meet them at the road-side, bowing to them as they came.
But the moving horsemen did not hear that I spoke the Han tongue:
Their Captain took me for a Tartar born and had me bound in
   chains.
They are sending me away to the south-east, to a low and swampy
   land:
No one now will take pity on me: resistance is all in vain.
Thinking of this, my voice chokes and I ask of Heaven above
Was I spared from death only to spend the rest of my years in sorrow?
My native village of Liang-yüan I shall not see again:
My wife and children in the Tartars' land I have fruitlessly deserted.

When I fell among Tartars and was taken prisoner, I pined for the
  land of Han:
Now that I am back in the land of Han, they have turned me into
  a Tartar.
Had I but known what my fate would be, I would not have started
  home!
For the two lands, so wide apart, are alike in the sorrow they bring.
                    Tartar prisoners in chains!
Of all the sorrows of all the prisoners mine is the hardest to bear!
Never in the world has so great a wrong befallen the lot of man,—
A Han heart and a Han tongue set in the body of a Turk."

RICHARD CHURCH b. 1893

from

TWENTIETH CENTURY PSALTER

TWENTY-FOURTH DAY—EVENING

If, when the century is done,
I shall be living still,
A centenarian whose chill
Blood in a trickle, frail and thin,
Creeps from vein to vein, each one
A monument above the skin,
I shall have known, maybe forgotten,
Two world-disconcerting wars.
Save for some intellectual scars
I shall remain unmoved
By what those conflicts proved.

On the warm sunside of a wall,
Beneath the willow whose trunk grows rotten,
Sheltered to eastward by the quince
Aged, over-rough and arid since
Its harvest-home of irony,
I may babble and recall
A tyrant's end, an empire's fall.

More likely I shall turn an eye
To nearer things, to further things,
Mysteries of age and infancy,
Some elements that have remained
Unmastered, unexplained;
The sparrow's nature, the vermin's worth
The mirage beauty makes when youth
Burns with desire and calls it truth,
A mother's voice that haunts
The century through, but cannot tell
What desperate thing it wants.
I, from my soul, as from a well
Disused and deep, shall draw with mirth
These words on which wise men may dwell.
'I am a stranger upon earth.'

MATTHEW ARNOLD 1822-1888

THE LAST WORD

Creep into thy narrow bed,
Creep, and let no more be said!
Vain, thy onset! All stands fast;
Thou thyself must break at last.

Let the long contention cease!
Geese are swans, and swans are geese.
Let them have it how they will!
Thou art tired; best be still!

They out-talked thee, hiss'd thee, tore thee.
Better men fared thus before thee;
Fired their ringing shot and pass'd,
Hotly charged — and broke at last.

Charge once more, then, and be dumb!
Let the victors, when they come,
When the forts of folly fall,
Find thy body by the wall.

ANONYMOUS

THE FORT OF RATHANGAN

The fort over against the oak-wood,
Once it was Bruidge's, it was Cathal's
It was Aed's, it was Ailill's,
It was Conaing's, it was Cuiline's,
And it was Maelduin's;
The fort remains after each in his turn—
And the kings asleep in the ground.

A. H. CLOUGH 1819-1861

from

AMOURS DE VOYAGE

Victory! Victory! — Yes! ah, yes, thou republican Zion,
Truly the kings of the earth are gathered and gone by together;
Doubtless they marvelled to witness such things, were astonished,
   and so forth.
Victory! Victory! Victory! — Ah, but it is, believe me,
Easier, easier far, to intone the chant of the martyr
Than to indite any pæan of any victory. Death may
Sometimes be noble; but life, at the best, will appear an illusion.
While the great pain is upon us, it is great; when it is over,
Why, it is over. The smoke of the sacrifice rises to heaven,
Of a sweet savour, no doubt, to Somebody; but on the altar,
Lo, there is nothing remaining but ashes and dirt and ill odour.
So it stands, you perceive; the labial muscles that swelled with
Vehement evolution of yesterday Marseillaises,
Articulations sublime of defiance and scorning, to-day col-
Lapse and languidly mumble, while men and women and papers
Scream and re-scream to each other the chorus of Victory. Well, but
I am thankful they fought, and glad that the Frenchmen were beaten.

DAVID GASCOYNE b.1919

SONNET

THE UNCERTAIN BATTLE

Away the horde rode, in a storm of hail
And steel-blue lightning. Hurtled by the wind
Into their eardrums from behind the hill
Came in increasing bursts the startled sound
Of trumpets in the unseen hostile camp.—
Down through a raw black hole in heaven stared
The horror-blanched moon's eye. Across the swamp
Five ravens flapped; and the storm disappeared
Soon afterwards, like them, into that pit
Of Silence which lies waiting to consume
Even the braggart World itself at last . . .
The candle in the hermit's cave burned out
At dawn, as usual. — No-one ever came
Back down the hill, to say which side had lost.

WALTER DE LA MARE b. 1873

THE SONG OF SOLDIERS

As I sat musing by the frozen dyke,
There was one man marching with a bright steel pike,
Marching in the dayshine like a ghost came he,
And behind me was the moaning and the murmur of the sea.

As I sat musing, 'twas not one but ten—
Rank on rank of ghostly soldiers marching o'er the fen,
Marching in the misty air they showed in dreams to me,
And behind me was the shouting and the shattering of the sea.

As I sat musing, 'twas a host in dark array,
With their horses and their cannon wheeling onward to the fray,
Moving like a shadow to the fate the brave must dree,
And behind me roared the drums, rang the trumpets of the sea.

IX

GEORGE WILLIAM RUSSELL (A.E.) 1867-1935
MUTINY

That blazing galleon the sun,
This dusky coracle I ride,
Both under secret orders sail,
And swim upon the selfsame tide.

The fleet of stars, my boat of soul,
By perilous magic mountains pass,
Or lie where no horizons gleam
Fainting upon a sea of glass.

Come, break the seals and tell us now
Upon what enterprise we roam:
To storm what city of the gods
Or — sail for the green fields of home.

W. J. TURNER b. 1889
THE HERO

To be brave is not enough,
It is not enough to be rough;
To be smooth is not enough,
Cunning is not enough;
It is not enough to know the truth.
Vengeance is not enough,
Pity is not enough, nor is ruth,
Ruthlessness is not enough
Even righteousness does not make a man of worth.
The way of salvation is a hard and narrow path,
Devious and hidden,
It is not disclosed to him who does what he is bidden;
Even constant persistence
Along the line of most resistance
Is not enough, is not enough.

He who would be a hero let him weep,
But for others, not for himself.
Upright, he must also know how to creep,
He does not even trust the secret passion in his heart;
He knows that to be a hero
Is like the mathematical zero.
In itself it is nothing but it multiplies by ten
The virtues of *other* men.
He must be so sane that he may appear mad,
So good that he may often appear bad,
So ordinary that nobody knows that it is he;
For he is only the man that everybody would be
If he followed the secret passion in his heart:
And ever, inwardly, in compassion,
Let him weep, let him weep.

WALT WHITMAN 1819-1892
RECONCILIATION

Word over all, beautiful as the sky,
Beautiful that war, and all its deeds of carnage must in time be utterly lost,
That the hands of the sisters Death and Night incessantly
Softly wash again, and ever again, this soiled world;
For my enemy is dead — a man divine as myself is dead.
I look where he lies, white-faced and still, in the coffin—I draw near,
I bend down and touch lightly with my lips the white face in the coffin.

A. E. HOUSMAN 1858-1936
SOLDIER FROM THE WARS RETURNING

Soldier from the wars returning,
    Spoiler of the taken town,
Here is ease that asks not earning;
    Turn you in and sit you down.

Peace is come and wars are over,
    Welcome you and welcome all,
While the charger crops the clover
    And his bridle hangs in stall.

Now no more of winters biting,
    Filth in trench from fall to spring,
Summers full of sweat and fighting
    For the Kesar or the King.

Rest you, charger, rust you, bridle;
    Kings and kesars, keep your pay;
Soldier set you down and idle
    At the inn of night for aye.

SAMUEL TAYLOR COLERIDGE 1772-1834

from

THE PICCOLOMINI

'Twas the first leisure of my life. O tell me,
What is the meed and purpose of the toil,
The painful toil, which robbed me of my youth,
Left me a heart unsoul'd and solitary,
A spirit uninformed, unornamented.
For the camp's stir and crowd and ceaseless larum,
The neighing war-horse, the air-shattering trumpet,
The unvaried, still-returning hour of duty,
Word of command, and exercise of arms—
There's nothing here, there's nothing in all this
To satisfy the heart, the gasping heart!
Mere bustling nothingness, where the soul is not—
This cannot be the sole felicity,
These cannot be man's best and only pleasures...
O! day thrice lovely! when at length the soldier
Returns home into life; when he becomes
A fellow-man among his fellow-men.
The colours are unfurled, the cavalcade
Marshals, and now the buzz is hushed, and hark!
Now the soft peace-march beats, home, brothers, home!
The caps and helmets are all garlanded
With green boughs, the last plundering of the fields.
The city gates fly open of themselves,
They need no longer the petard to tear them.
The ramparts are all filled with men and women,
With peaceful men and women, that send onwards
Kisses and welcomings upon the air,
Which they make breezy with affectionate gestures.
From all the towers rings out the merry peal,
The joyous vespers of a bloody day.
O happy man, O fortunate! for whom
The well-known door, the faithful arms are open,
The faithful tender arms with mute embracing.

JOHN CLARE 1793 - 1864

THE RETURNED SOLDIER

The soldier, full of battles and renown,
And gaping wonder of each quiet lown,
And strange to every face he knew so well,
Comes once again in this old town to dwell.
But man alone is changed; the very tree
He sees again where once he used to swee;
And the old fields where once he tented sheep,
And the old mole-hills where he used to leap,
And the old bush where once he found a nest
Are just the same, and pleasure fills his breast.
He sees the old path where he used to play
At chock and marbles many a summer day,
And loves to wander where he went a boy,
And fills his heart with pleasure and with joy.

PATRIC DICKINSON b. 1914

WORLD WITHOUT END

A world is breaking. Midnight's bell rings down
The fable-founded stones of palace walls;
The swallows and the merchants all are flown,
The rooftree of the temple rocks and falls.
Yet peopled is the fallen mart and court,
The altar served whatever ill be done;
The forms of man's unalterable thought
Carve still their timeless perfect Parthenon.

Age cools the fevered stars: they fall, they die.
Stone crumbles, iron rusts, to thankful rest:
Man's spirit rooted in eternity
Beats on inviolate within the breast
Of time, and grows not cold nor hard nor old,
Whatever cloaks of flesh impede and mar,
Building anew each towering-tumbling world
From dust, from fallen star.

PERCY BYSSHE SHELLEY 1792-1822

THE WORLD'S GREAT AGE BEGINS ANEW

    The world's great age begins anew,
      The golden years return,
    The earth doth like a snake renew
      Her winter weeds outworn:
    Heaven smiles, and faiths and empires gleam,
    Like wrecks of a dissolving dream.

    A brighter Hellas rears its mountains
      From waves serener far;
    A new Peneus rolls his fountains
      Against the morning-star.
    Where fairer Tempes bloom, there sleep
    Young Cyclads on a sunnier deep.

    A loftier Argo cleaves the main,
      Fraught with a later prize;
    Another Orpheus sings again,
      And loves, and weeps, and dies;
    A new Ulysses leaves once more
    Calypso for his native shore.

    Oh, write no more the tale of Troy,
      If earth Death's scroll must be!
    Nor mix with Laian rage the joy
      Which dawns upon the free:
    Although a subtler Sphinx renew
    Riddles of death Thebes never knew.

    Another Athens shall arise,
      And to remoter time
    Bequeath, like sunset to the skies,
      The splendour of its prime;
    And leave, if nought so bright may live,
    All earth can take or Heaven can give.

Saturn and Love their long repose
    Shall burst, more bright and good
Than all who fell, than One who rose,
    Than many unsubdued:
Not gold, not blood, their altar dowers,
But votive tears and symbol flowers.

Oh, cease! must hate and death return?
    Cease! must men kill and die?
Cease! drain not to its dregs the urn
    Of bitter prophecy.
The world is weary of the past,
Oh, might it die or rest at last!

ACKNOWLEDGMENTS

"O WHAT IS THAT SOUND WHICH SO THRILLS THE EAR" and "REFUGEE BLUES" are reprinted from *Look Stranger* and *Another Time* by W. H. Auden by courtesy of Faber & Faber Ltd.; "THE PACIFIST" from *Sonnets and Verse* (Duckworth) by Hilaire Belloc by courtesy of the Author; "THE MEMORIAL, 1914-1918" and "SOME TALK OF PEACE" from *Poems 1930-1940* (Macmillan) by Edmund Blunden by courtesy of the Author; "GIBRALTAR" from *Collected Poems* by W. S. Blunt by courtesy of Macmillan & Co. Ltd.; "HIALMAR" from *Adamastor* by Roy Campbell by courtesy of Faber & Faber Ltd.; "ELEGY IN A COUNTRY CHURCHYARD" from *The Collected Poems of G. K. Chesterton* by courtesy of Miss Collins and Methuen & Co.; Extract from *Twentieth Century Psalter* (Dent) by Richard Church by courtesy of the Author; "KEEP INNOCENCY", "NAPOLEON", "THE OLD SOLDIER" and "THE SONG OF SOLDIERS" all by Walter de la Mare by courtesy of the Author; "TRIUMPHAL MARCH" from *Collected Poems* by T. S. Eliot by courtesy of Faber & Faber Ltd.; "TAOPING" from *Collected Poems* by James Elroy Flecker by courtesy of Martin Secker & Warburg Ltd.; "RANGE-FINDING" and "A SOLDIER" from *Collected Poems* by Robert Frost by courtesy of Jonathan Cape, Ltd.; "THE MODERN MAJOR-GENERAL" from *Pirates of Penzance* by Sir W. S. Gilbert by courtesy of Miss Nancy McIntosh and Macmillan & Co. Ltd.; "THE UNCERTAIN BATTLE" from *Poems 1937-1942* (Nicholson & Watson) by David Gascoyne by courtesy of the Author; "APOLLYON" from *Apollyon and other Poems* (Heinemann) by George Rostrevor Hamilton by courtesy of the Author; "MEN WHO MARCH AWAY" and "THE MAN HE KILLED" from *The Collected Poems of Thomas Hardy* by courtesy of the Hardy Estate and Macmillan & Co. Ltd.; "THE STREET SOUNDS TO THE SOLDIERS' TREAD", "IN VALLEYS GREEN AND STILL" and "SOLDIER FROM THE WARS RETURNING" all from *Collected Poems* by A. E. Housman by courtesy of The Society of Authors on behalf of the Trustees of the Estate of the late A. E. Housman and Jonathan Cape, Ltd.; "THE COMING OF WAR" and "CHILD OF WAR" from *The Poetical Works of Lionel Johnson* by courtesy of George Allen & Unwin, Ltd.; "ADVICE FOR A JOURNEY" from *Collected Poems of Sidney Keyes* by courtesy of George Routledge & Sons, Ltd.; "THE BRIDEGROOM" and "MESOPOTAMIA, 1917" from *The Years Between* by Rudyard Kipling by courtesy of Mrs. Bambridge and Messrs. Methuen; "AFTER DUNKIRK" and "ON A BEREAVED GIRL" from *Raiders Dawn* by Alun Lewis by courtesy of George Allen & Unwin, Ltd.; "THE STAND-TO" from *Word over All* by Cecil Day Lewis by courtesy of the Author and Jonathan Cape, Ltd.; "COELO TONANTEM" translated by Sir Edward Marsh by courtesy of the Author; "IN FLANDERS FIELDS" by John McCrae by courtesy of the Proprietors of *Punch*; "SUMMER IN ENGLAND" by Alice Meynell by courtesy of Wilfrid Meynell; "THE NON-COMBATANT" from *Poems New and Old* (John Murray) by Sir Henry Newbolt by courtesy of Captain Francis Newbolt; "THE SENTRY" and "FUTILITY" by Wilfred Owen from *Collected Poems* by courtesy of Messrs. Chatto & Windus; "THE CAMPAIGN" from *Chosen Poems* by Frederic Prokosch by courtesy of Messrs. Chatto & Windus; "LOST IN FRANCE" by Ernest Rhys by courtesy of the Author; "DUNKIRK PIER" from *Soldiers this Solitude* by Alan Rook by courtesy of the Author and George Routledge & Sons Ltd.; "MUTINY" from *Collected Poems* by George Russell (A.E.) by courtesy of Macmillan & Co. Ltd.; "ANCIENT HISTORY",

"Dreamers" and "Does it Matter" by Siegfried Sassoon by courtesy of the Author; "I have a rendezvous with Death" from *Poems by Alan Seeger* by courtesy of Constable & Co. Ltd.; "All the Hills and Vales Among" from *Marlborough and other Poems* by C. H. Sorley by courtesy of the Cambridge University Press; "Ultima Ratio Regum" from *The Still Centre* by Stephen Spender by courtesy of Faber & Faber, Ltd.; "The Death of a Soldier" by Wallace Stevens by courtesy of Alfred Knopf, Inc.; "The Hand that signed the Paper felled a City" from *Twenty-five Poems* (Dent) by Dylan Thomas by courtesy of the Author; "A Private", "In Memoriam (Easter 1915)" and "This is no Case of Petty Right and Wrong" from *Collected Poems* (Faber & Faber) by Edward Thomas by courtesy of Mrs. Helen Thomas; "Talking with Soldiers" and "The Hero" by W. J. Turner by courtesy of the Author; "The Scholar Recruit", "Fighting south of the Castle" and "The Prisoner" from *100 Chinese Poems* translated by Arthur Waley by courtesy of the Author and Constable & Co.; "Penelope" by Ursula Wood by courtesy of the Author; "The Road at my Door" by W. B. Yeats by courtesy of Mrs. Yeats and Macmillan & Co. Ltd.

INDEX

	PAGE
ANONYMOUS	
An Old Souldier of the Queens	90
The Fort of Rathangan	104
ARNOLD, MATTHEW 1822-1888	
The Last Word	104
AUDEN, W. H. b.1907	
O what is that Sound which so thrills the Ear	14
Refugee Blues	99
AYTOUN, W. E. 1813-1865	
Sonnet to Britain	81
BELLOC, HILAIRE b.1870	
The Pacifist	1
BLUNDEN, EDMUND b.1896	
The Memorial, 1914-1918	64
Some Talk of Peace	97
BLUNT, WILFRED SCAWEN 1840-1922	
Gibraltar	20
BROWNING, ROBERT 1812-1889	
Incident of the French Camp	78
BYRON, LORD 1788-1824	
Stanzas	68
CAMPBELL, ROY b.1902	
Hialmar	47
CHESTERTON, G. K. 1874-1936	
Elegy in a Country Churchyard	66
CHURCH, RICHARD b.1893	
Twentieth Century Psalter, *extract*	103
CLARE, JOHN 1793-1864	
The Soldier	25
The Returned Soldier	112
CLOUGH, A. H. 1819-1861	
Amours de Voyage, *extracts*	2, 4, 12, 33, 105
COLERIDGE, SAMUEL TAYLOR 1772-1834	
Fears in Solitude	70
The Piccolomini, *extract*	111
DAVISON, EDWARD L.	
Nocturne	62
DE LA MARE, WALTER b.1873	
Keep Innocency	51
Napoleon	77

	PAGE
The Old Soldier	89
The Song of Soldiers	107
DICKINSON, PATRIC b.1914	
War	52
World Without End	113
ELIOT, T. S. b.1888	
Triumphal March	84
FLECKER, JAMES ELROY 1884-1915	
Taoping	35
FROST, ROBERT b.1875	
Range-Finding	29
A Soldier	58
GILBERT, W. S. 1836-1911	
The Modern Major-General	91
GASCOYNE, DAVID b.1919	
The Uncertain Battle	106
HAMILTON, G. ROSTREVOR b.1888	
Apollyon	94
HARDY, THOMAS 1840-1928	
Men Who March Away	18
The Man he Killed	46
HOOD, THOMAS 1799-1845	
Faithless Nellie Gray	44
HOUSMAN, A. E. 1859-1936	
The Street Sounds to the Soldiers' Tread	13
In Valleys Green and Still	16
Soldier from the Wars Returning	110
JOHNSON, LIONEL 1867-1902	
The Coming of War, 1889	9
Child of War	39
KEYES, SIDNEY 1922-1943	
Advice for a Journey	3
KIPLING, RUDYARD 1865-1936	
The Bridegroom	17
Mesopotamia, 1917	66
LANDOR, WALTER SAVAGE 1775-1864	
A Foreign Ruler	77
LEWIS, ALUN 1920-1944	
After Dunkirk	49
On a Bereaved Girl	60

	PAGE
LEWIS, C. DAY b.1904	
The Stand-To	30
MARSH, SIR EDWARD	
Coelo Tonantem from the Latin of Horace. Odes III, 5	86
MCCRAE, JOHN	
In Flanders Fields	60
MELVILLE, HERMAN 1819-1891	
Ball's Bluff	22
Shiloh	38
On the Home Guards	59
MEREDITH, GEORGE 1828-1909	
"Atkins"	14
MEYNELL, ALICE 1847-1922	
Summer in England, 1914	41
MORRIS, WILLIAM 1834-1896	
The Judgment of God	26
The Knight in Prison	40
NEWBOLT, SIR HENRY 1862-1938	
The Non-Combatant	2
OWEN, WILFRED 1893-1918	
The Sentry	42
Futility	63
PEACOCK, THOMAS LOVE 1785-1866	
The War Song of Dinas Vawr	37
PROKOSCH, FREDERIC b.1909	
The Campaign	32
PRAED, WINTHROP MACKWORTH 1802-1839	
Waterloo	82
RHYS, ERNEST b.1859	
Lost in France	57
ROOK, ALAN b.1913	
Dunkirk Pier	69
RUSSELL, GEORGE WILLIAM (A.E.) 1867-1935	
Mutiny	107
SASSOON, SIEGFRIED b.1886	
Ancient History	1
Dreamers	13
Does it Matter	43
SEEGER, ALAN 1888-1916	
I have a Rendezvous with Death	11
SHANNON, SHEILA b.1913	
Soldier and Girl Sleeping	23

	PAGE
SHELLEY, PERCY BYSSHE 1792-1822	
The World's Great Age Begins Anew	114
SORLEY, C. H. 1895-1915	
All the Hills and Vales Along	20
SOUTHEY, ROBERT 1774-1843	
The Battle of Blenheim	53
SPENDER, STEPHEN b.1909	
Ultima Ratio Regum	52
STEVENS, WALLACE b.1879	
The Death of a Soldier	56
STEVENSON, R. L. 1850-1894	
A Martial Elegy for some lead Soldiers	79
TENNYSON, ALFRED LORD 1809-1892	
To General Hamley	88
THOMAS, DYLAN b.1914	
The Hand that signed the Paper felled a City	65
THOMAS, EDWARD 1878-1917	
A Private	57
In Memoriam (Easter 1915)	58
This is no Case of petty Right or Wrong	68
TURNER, W. J. b.1889	
Talking with Soldiers	97
The Hero	109
WALEY, ARTHUR	
The Scholar Recruit	18
Translated from the Chinese of Pao Chao d. 466. A.D.	
Fighting South of the Castle	34
Translated from the Chinese	
The Prisoner	100
Translated from the Chinese	
WHITMAN, WALT 1819-1892	
Manhattan Arming	5
A Sight in Camp	59
Reconciliation	110
WOOD, URSULA b.1911	
Penelope	24
WORDSWORTH, WILLIAM 1770-1850	
Sonnet Composed in 1811	8
The French and Spanish Guerrillas	31
November 1806	67
Sonnet on the Column intended by Buonepart for a Triumphal Edifice in Milan	80
YEATS, W. B. 1865-1939	
The Road at my Door	93

6665 032